Removing Disabling Barriers

Ed:

POLIC
Londo

PUBLISHING

The publishing imprint of the independent
POLICY STUDIES INSTITUTE
100 Park Village East, London NW1 3SR
Telephone: 0171 468 0468   Fax: 0171 388 0914

© **Policy Studies Institute 1995**

ISBN 0 85374 667 2

PSI Research Report 805

A CIP catalogue record of this book is available from the British Library.

1 2 3 4 5 6 7 8 9

PSI publications are available from
BEBC Distribution Ltd
P O Box 1496, Poole, Dorset, BH12 3YD

Books will normally be despatched within 24 hours. Cheques should be made payable to BEBC Distribution Ltd.

Credit card and telephone/fax orders may be placed on the following freephone numbers:

FREEPHONE: 0800 262260
FREEFAX: 0800 262266

Booktrade representation (UK & Eire):
Broadcast Books
24 De Montfort Road, London SW16 1LW
Telephone: 0181 677 5129

PSI subscriptions are available from PSI's subscription agent
Carfax Publishing Company Ltd
P O Box 25, Abingdon, Oxford OX14 3UE

Laserset by Policy Studies Institute
Printed in Great Britain by Redwood Books, Trowbridge, Wiltshire

Contents

About the contributors

Len Barton is Professor of Education at the University of Sheffield. He is also chair of the *British Journal of Sociology of Education* and editor of the international journal *Disability and Society*. His numerous publications in the fields of education and disability include *The Politics of Special Needs, Disability and Dependency*, and *Special Education: Policy, Practice and Social Issues* (with Sally Tomlinson).

Richard Berthoud is a Senior Fellow at the Policy Studies Institute. He has published widely in the area of social security, poverty and social policy and has a particular interest in income and disability. His recent publications include *Credit and Debt in Britain* (with Elaine Kempson), *Invalidity Benefit: Where Will the Savings Come From?*, and *The Economic Problems of Disabled People* (with Jane Lakey and Stephen McKay).

Marca Bristo is Chair of the United States Council on Disability – a Federal Agency which serves to monitor and advise on the implementation of disabled people's civil rights – and was the first disabled person appointed by President Clinton. She is also President of the Chicago Centre for Independent Living. She has been a leading figure in the American disability movement and the campaign for civil rights for people with disabilities. She was also closely involved in the drafting of the Americans with Disabilities Act.

Ian Bynoe is a solicitor and former Legal Director of MIND. He is currently a Research Fellow at the Institute for Public Policy Research. He has an extensive knowledge of the legal aspects of disability and discrimination, both in the UK and other countries. His publications include *Equal Rights for Disabled People: The Case for a New Law* (with Mike Oliver and Colin Barnes)

Clare Evans is the Convenor of the Wiltshire Users Network – an independent group (supported by the local authority) which serves to ensure that disabled people are represented and involved in local service planning.

She has also been involved in a number of initiatives in developing user-led services.

Bob Findlay is vice-chair of the British Council of Organisations of Disabled People and Director of Birmingham Action on Disability (formerly Birmingham Disability Rights). He has been active in the disability movement for a number of years and has also recently been involved with the development of the National Disability Information Project.

Caroline Gooding is Employment Officer at the Royal Association for Disability and Rehabilitation. Formerly a solicitor at the Disability Law Service, she received a Fulbright Scholarship to study American Civil Rights and Disability Legislation for an LLM at University of California at Berkeley. The results of this study are published in the forthcoming book: *Disabling Laws, Enabling Acts.*

Bryan Heiser is Director of Central London Dial-A-Ride and a Policy Officer in LB of Camden. He has carried out research on transport and housing issues and was co-author of the recent report on *Cross-Sector Benefits of Accessible Public Transport* produced by the Cranfield University School of Management.

Dr Ray Jones is Director of Wiltshire Social Services and a member of the Association of Directors of Social Services Disabilities Committee. He has considerable knowledge of the operation of disability policies from a local authority perspective and has also been active in supporting the development of user-led services.

Mike Oliver is Professor of Disability Studies at the University of Greenwich. He is an internationally recognised academic and political commentator and has published numerous books and articles on disability and other social policy issues over the last 15 years. His recent publications include *The Politics of Disablement,* and *Discrimination, Disability and Welfare* (with Colin Barnes). He is also a co-editor of the Open University course reader – *Disabling Barriers – Enabling Environments.*

Rachel Hurst is Project Director of Disability Awareness in Action – an international public education campaign established to support, promote and co-ordinate national action by disabled peoples' organisations and their allies, and to further the equalisation of opportunities and rights of all disabled people in accordance with the 1983 UN World Programme of Action Concerning Disabled Persons. In a voluntary capacity, Rachel Hurst is chair of the Disabled Peoples International/European Union Committee and, in the past, has also been chair of the British Council of Organisations of Disabled People and a founding member of one of the first Centres for Independent Living in the UK. She has recently been awarded an OBE for her services to disabled people.

Andrew Walker AA Dipl, RIBA, Grad Dipl Cons (AA) is Head of Environmental Access and Technical Studies at the Architectural Association School of Architecture. He is also Consultant Architect to ASPIRE and a member of the European Institute for Design and Disability, the British Film Institute Disability Committee, and the Joseph Rowntree Foundation Lifetime Homes Group. He was formerly an Access Officer for LB of Harrow and the Honorary Secretary of the Access Officers Association in its inaugural year.

Gerry Zarb is a Senior Fellow and leader of the Disability Programme at PSI. He has carried out a number of research projects on disability issues including independent living; the costs and benefits of cash payments for personal assistance; participation of disabled people in training and employment; ageing and disability; access to health services; and, the take-up of Disability Working Allowance. He is currently leading a major ESRC funded study on measuring disablement in society. Recent publications include *Ageing with a Disability: What do they expect after all these years?* (with Mike Oliver) and *Cashing in on Independence: Comparing the costs and benefits of cash and services* (with Pamela Nadash).

Part One

Introduction

1   Removing disabling barriers: an overview

Gerry Zarb

Current debates about the nature of disablement in society are increasingly focused on discrimination and the redefinition of disability as a civil rights issue. This publication collects together the papers presented at the *Removing Disabling Barriers* conference held at PSI in September 1994. The aim of this publication is to draw together the evidence on the extent and causes of discrimination and disadvantage faced by disabled people, and to examine the policy options for removing the barriers to disabled people's participation in social and economic life from a range of local, national and international perspectives.

In particular, the publication examines the case for comprehensive civil rights legislation along the lines of the Americans with Disabilities Act and how this compares to the more limited measures proposed in the UK government's recent Disability Discrimination Bill. The various papers contained in this publication also look at some of the practical issues involved in putting anti-discrimination legislation into practice.

In order to examine these issues from a variety of perspectives, we have tried to bring together a range of views from researchers and academics and from within the disability movement itself. This has, of necessity, meant that the various papers in this publication exhibit a mix of content and style ranging from the philosophical and polemic to the academic and analytical. Also, given that the conference was held against the background of an ongoing political – and often controversial – campaign around the implementation of anti-discrimination legislation, it is not surprising that the debate was sometimes quite politically charged and this also is reflected in one or two of the papers. However, given the significance of the debate on anti-discrimination legislation, it is obviously important to try to ensure that all the relevant issues and views are expressed.

The *Removing Disabling Barriers* conference was organised as part of a major research project on *Measuring Disablement in Society* being carried out by the Policy Studies Institute in association with Colin Barnes at the Disability Research Unit, University of Leeds. The project, which is funded by the Economic and Social Research Council, aims to undertake a systematic examination of the obstacles to disabled people's full participation in society. It will provide evidence on the physical, social and economic barriers faced by disabled people and – for the first time – attempt to demonstrate how such barriers can be measured. The issues raised during the conference will, therefore, make an important contribution to the development of this project.

The nature of disabling barriers

There are many different types of barrier which prevent disabled people's full and equal participation in society: not only physical barriers created by lack of access to buildings and transport systems, but also social and economic barriers resulting from unequal access to education, employment and services; lack of representation and involvement in local planning and politics; and a limited understanding of the nature of disablement.

It is now widely recognised that many disabled people face direct or indirect discrimination as a result of these barriers. The United Nations *World Programme of Action Concerning Disabled Persons* has the stated objective of promoting equal opportunities for disabled citizens in all areas of economic and social life. Several countries have now adopted a variety of measures aimed at putting this into practice. The most far-reaching of these measures has been the recent introduction of comprehensive anti-discrimination legislation in the United States.

At a local level, many local authorities are also looking much more closely at their own policies on disability equality in the light of the community care reforms and, in particular, the *Citizen's Charter*.

This growing recognition of discrimination, combined with pressure from disabled people's organisations and their supporters, has made the prospect of some form of anti-discrimination legislation in Britain increasingly likely. However, there is still a considerable amount of disagreement about what form this legislation should take, how much it would cost and how far it will go towards establishing and protecting comprehensive rights for disabled people.

The recent *Civil Rights (Disabled Persons) Bill*, which would have introduced comprehensive protection against discrimination, has been rejected by the government. The main reasons given for rejecting the Bill were: first, that the legislation would have been too complex to implement and monitor; and, second, that the costs, most of which would have to be met by business and employers, would have a damaging effect on Britain's international competitiveness. The argument about costs has been particularly contentious with a wide variety of estimates being produced at different times and by different groups involved in the debate.

Following the publication of a consultation document on proposed measures to tackle discrimination, the government subsequently introduced its own *Disability Discrimination Bill* which now seems almost certain to become law, if not by the time this book is published, then certainly before the end of 1995. Although some concessions to the demands of the disability lobby are quite likely to have been included by the time it is passed, the measures contained in the new legislation are not intended to be anywhere near as far-ranging as those proposed in the Civil Rights Bill. Instead, the government proposes a combination of education and persuasion, self-regulation, and limited and closely targeted legislation such as a new law to replace the employment quota scheme.

These measures have been criticised for being too limited and piecemeal, and for failing to protect disabled people's rights. As a result they have only led to renewed pressure to implement comprehensive anti-discrimination legislation along the same lines as the *Americans with Disabilities Act*.

It was against this background that PSI organised a major two day conference which offered participants the opportunity to contribute to the important debate about the future direction of measures to tackle discrimination against disabled people. The aim of the conference was not so much to establish whether or not there is a need for legislation, but rather to examine what form such legislation might take.

In Chapter 2 Mike Oliver looks at the question of how far anti-discrimination legislation can be seen as the solution to protecting the rights of disabled people, and examines the prospects for the extension of these rights in the future.

The next six chapters look in detail at the different forms of discrimination faced by disabled people in the areas of education, access and transport, employment, and economic disadvantage. Each of these chapters examines the evidence on the particular barriers created in these areas, and discusses some of the specific measures that might be necessary to remove them.

In Chapter 3 Len Barton examines the issues around discrimination in education. The chapter contrasts the development of inclusive and segregationist education policies and the impact these have had on disabled people's rights. The following two chapters by Andrew Walker and Bryan Heiser examine the evidence on access barriers in the built environment and transport systems and explore some of the ways in which these might be removed.

The last two chapters in this section of the book explore issues around employment and the financial circumstances of disabled people. In Chapter 6, Caroline Gooding contrasts different legislative approaches to tackling discrimination in employment and examines which of these might offer the best solution for extending equal opportunities and rights for disabled people. Finally, in Chapter 7 Richard Berthoud examines the financial circumstances of disabled people and the extra costs associated with disability. In particular, the chapter looks at the operation of the social security system as a mechanism for tackling the financial difficulties faced by many disabled people and identifies some of the most important areas which future policy developments might need to address.

The next set of chapters takes a wider view of the policy options for tackling discrimination and examine how these might be translated into legislation. In Chapter 8 Rachel Hurst examines the different forms which discrimination against disabled people takes in various regions of the world from both a historical and contemporary perspective. She goes on to discuss the kinds of solution which are proposed at an international level and the prospects these offer for ending discrimination and extending disabled people's human and civil rights. The paper by Marca Bristo which follows offers an insight into the operation of the Americans with Disabilities Act and discusses the lessons that might be learned for developing anti-discrimination in the UK.

Chapters 10 and 11 switch the focus away from activities at the international level to look at some of the ways in which the barriers to disabled people's participation can be tackled at a local level and, in particular, the important role which organisations of disabled people can play in this. First Ray Jones examines the existing legislative context provided by the 1970 Chronically Sick and Disabled Persons Act, the 1986 Disabled Persons (Services, Consultation and

Representation) Act and the 1990 National Health Service and Community Care Act, and the obligations and opportunities these create for local authorities to promote equality for disabled people at a local level. In the next chapter Clare Evans looks at the same issues from the perspective of disabled people themselves. In particular, she examines the issues around funding and enabling representative disability and user groups as active participants in the development of local policies and services. She also explores the impact which such groups have had on the creation of services run and controlled by disabled people themselves.

In Chapter 12, Ian Bynoe considers how discrimination is treated in the present legal system and the implications this would have for any legislation that might be adopted in the future. In particular, he examines how different forms of direct and indirect discrimination are defined in law and the potential complexities in framing comprehensive anti-discrimination legislation which can encompass these different forms of discrimination effectively.

In the final chapter, Bob Findlay looks at the development of the disability movements campaign for civil rights, the impact this has had on debates about the need for anti-discrimination legislation, and what the movement hopes this will achieve in the future.

Prospects for removing disabling barriers

Although the chapters in this publication examine disabling barriers and anti-discrimination from a variety of different perspectives, a number of common themes can be identified.

First, the overall conclusions from the conference were mostly very positive about the prospects for removing the barriers to disabled people's full participation in society. At the same time, the extent to which these prospects can be realised – and how quickly the barriers removed – is also seen to depend on whether future policies are framed by a civil rights or an anti-discrimination perspective. As all the chapters illustrate, there are in fact some crucial distinctions between these two perspectives, not only in terms of the kinds of solutions they propose, but also in relation to the scope they offer for extending the rights of disabled people.

In particular, while the civil rights approach is seen as a vehicle for creating opportunities for disabled people to become full and active members of society, the anti-discrimination approach is seen as being limited simply to protecting them against acts of discrimination. Although the latter is obviously important, it does nevertheless represent an essentially neutral approach to rights. The kinds of measure proposed from a civil rights perspective, on the other hand, seek to go further by actively and positively promoting the right to, and the opportunities for, self-determination for disabled people.

Not surprisingly, therefore, the most optimistic messages from the various papers tend to be those which relate to the prospects for civil rights legislation (even though this may still be in the future), while the difficulties discussed are more often seen as being linked to the limitations of the anti-discrimination approach.

Second, nearly all of the papers emphasise that – whatever form it takes – anti-discrimination legislation is only a means to an end and cannot, by itself, provide all the solutions to removing the barriers to disabled people's full participation in society. As Mike Oliver points out, legislation is only the starting point. In many ways it is the process of implementation which will be the most important (and potentially, the most difficult) challenge to ending discrimination in practice. For example, the papers by Rachel Hurst, Ray Jones, Caroline Gooding and Ian Bynoe in particular identify the potential limitations of legislation not backed up by adequate enforcement measures, while the discussions during the conference itself also highlighted the need for adequate monitoring to ensure that the intended outcomes of any legislation can actually be delivered. Nevertheless, as the experience of the Americans with Disabilities Act demonstrates, legislation is still essential for creating both a legal and a moral mandate for tackling discrimination.

Third, some of the papers (particularly those by Mike Oliver, Rachel Hurst and Marca Bristo) highlight that anti-discrimination legislation will not reach all disabled people. Disabled people in the developing world, for example, have even more basic and immediate needs essential for their day to day survival. While the meeting of these needs is clearly linked to the issue of civil and human rights, it is unlikely that anti-discrimination legislation itself would be seen as the main priority at this particular stage. Rather, as Rachel Hurst points out, the prime motivation for disabled people in these areas of the world 'is to eat and stay alive'. Similarly, there are whole groups of disabled people throughout the world who are effectively disenfranchised through the processes of segregation and institutionalisation. Ironically, although these groups probably have the most to gain from anti-discrimination legislation, they are also the least likely to be able to exercise the rights which it would bring.

Fourth, the fact that anti-discrimination legislation may not directly address the discrimination faced by large numbers of disabled people also points to the need to develop wider solutions aimed at tackling the material and cultural barriers to inclusion and participation. Again, while the removal of barriers caused by economic and material deprivation is partly dependent on rights-based solutions, this link can only be maintained if disabled people are enabled and empowered to exercise their rights.

Some of the papers also highlight that addressing discrimination is equally dependent on the need for cultural change. Mike Oliver, for example, points out that disabled people are marginalised and their experience distorted by the cultural production of disablist and disabling media imagery; also, that this situation is perpetuated by the exclusion of disabled people from the process of mainstream cultural production. Similarly, Bob Findlay argues that the social construction of disabled people's passive and dependent identities at the cultural level serves to reinforce material barriers to inclusion; the removal of these barriers is, therefore, equally dependent on the creation of an alternative cultural identity which recognises discrimination as a fundamental part of disabled people's experiences.

A fifth and related theme running through several of the papers is the contrasts and similarities between anti-discrimination legislation and other rights and equalities policies. According to Caroline Gooding, for example, the proposed disability discrimination legislation has the same limitations as existing race and gender legislation in that it fails to acknowledge that discrimination is institutionalised in society. Rather, she suggests that the proposed legislation is premised on the assumption that society is basically neutral and that acts of discrimination are only random occurrences which can, therefore, be addressed by a combination of education and persuasion backed up where necessary by legislation. Again, this suggests that legislation on its own will not be sufficient to tackle institutionalised discrimination unless it is part of a wider process of political and cultural change.

Some of the papers also highlight the ways in which existing legislation (for example, the 1944 Disabled Persons (Employment) Act, the 1970 Chronically Sick and Disabled Persons Act and the 1986 Disabled Persons Act) has often had only a very limited impact on protecting people from discrimination. In particular, one of the reasons why existing legislation does not address discrimination very effectively is that its legal requirements can be enforced only at the discretion of the state. Prosecutions for failing to meet employment quotas, for example, can be brought only by the state and not by individual disabled people. Fully comprehensive civil rights legislation, on the other hand, enables individuals to seek redress for specific and personal acts of discrimination. Although, as Ian Bynoe points out, the effectiveness of this approach is also dependent on having a legal system which is geared up to handle such litigation both on an individual level and, in some cases, in the context of collective actions relating to specific forms of systematic discrimination experienced by particular groups.

Finally, several of the papers discuss the role of the disability movement as a force for political and cultural change. Whether at the international, national or local levels, organisations of disabled people have clearly had an increasing influence on defining the agendas of mainstream political and administrative institutions. At the same time, however, some of the papers strike a cautionary note about the limitations of these institutions as a vehicle for securing rights for disabled people, and the fact that disabled people are still significantly under-represented at all levels of national and local politics. (Although, as Mike Oliver points out, these concerns also reflect a more general disillusionment with politics and other public institutions and the effectiveness of the democratic process.) Some also highlight potential contradictions and tensions between short-term legislative gains and the broader agenda around full inclusion and comprehensive civil rights, and the views expressed during the conference itself indicate that these will not necessarily be easy to resolve.

In particular, the debate around this issue has highlighted the dilemmas – which are as much about political strategy as they are about social policy – posed by questions such as the definition of who should be included in the legislation; whether or not it will be possible to extend the scope of anti-discrimination measures after legislation is in place; how to arrive at acceptable and workable definitions of 'reasonable accommodations' to address the needs of disabled people; and, how long it would be reasonable to wait for accommodations required by the legislation to be enforced.

Key issues for the development of anti-discrimination legislation

The discussion so far has suggested that there are a number of potential obstacles to bringing about full political, cultural and economic inclusion of disabled people in society. At the same time, the various chapters in this publication also highlight the potential of anti-discrimination and civil rights legislation as a vehicle for tackling the barriers to inclusion and identify a number of specific solutions which could help to bring this about.

The first and perhaps the most important of these is the need to develop policies which take the goals of 'inclusion' and 'participation' as their starting point. As Marca Bristo points out in the context of developing the Americans with Disabilities Act, it is essential to be clear about the underlying first principles of any anti-discrimination measures before starting to develop the nuts and bolts of the legislation itself. In other words, the scope of the legislation has to be defined before the detail.

Similar points were raised in the context of discussions about the removal of particular types of disabling barriers. Andrew Walker, for example, highlights some of the ways in which easily avoided access barriers often result from the failure by architects and planners to adopt universal access as an integral objective for developing the built environment. Similarly, Len Barton points out that the implications of debates about special education go further than simply determining policies on segregation versus inclusion in schools; rather, the question of segregationist versus inclusive solutions in education may have an even greater relevance in signifying what kind of society people want to build.

Second, adopting the full inclusion and participation of disabled people as a defining principle for anti-discrimination legislation also requires an equally inclusive definition of what constitutes discrimination. As several of the papers point out, disabled people's experiences – including the experience of discrimination – come as a total package; such experience cannot be easily divided up and compartmentalised. Indeed, this is one of the most important reasons why the disability lobby has opposed attempts to leave certain areas of discrimination (for example, discrimination in education) out of the proposed anti-discrimination legislation.

The debates around the need to adopt a broad definition of discrimination which takes account of the multi-faceted experience of exclusion is closely linked to the question of how disability should be defined and, consequently, which groups of disabled people should come within the scope of any rights-based legislation.

This issue has proved to be particularly controversial in recent debates around anti-discrimination and civil rights legislation in the UK. The government has expressed concerns about the practical difficulties associated with attempting to implement legislation based on a broad definition of disability which, it is believed, would introduce an unacceptable degree of subjectivity into disputes about particular cases of discrimination. The government's preferred approach is to identify a specific list of conditions and impairments which would be used to define who is and is not covered by the conditions of the legislation. The disability lobby has opposed this on the grounds that it would inevitably lead to the arbitrary exclusion of individuals and groups who are just as likely to experience some form of discrimination, and that such an approach fails to take account of the social dimensions of discrimination.

The arguments and evidence presented in the following chapters tend to support the case for inclusive definitions of discrimination and disability. At the same time, the discussions during the conference itself highlighted the potential problem that a broad-ranging definition might obscure the specific forms of discrimination experienced by particular groups of disabled people. Similarly, there is always the potential difficulty that the removal of barriers for particular groups or circumstances might initially conflict with the solutions required for others. Attempting to narrow these definitions, on the other hand, carries the equal danger of compartmentalising people's experiences and diverting attention away from the collective rights of disabled people as a whole. Consequently, the challenge will be to ensure that the particular needs of all groups who are likely to be covered by the legislation are considered in order to produce workable and inclusive definitions of disability and discrimination.

Clearly this is a difficult issue which has not yet been fully resolved and – if the experience of implementing the Americans with Disabilities Act is anything to go by – will probably not be resolved until after the new legislation is in place. As Marca Bristo points out, the Americans with Disabilities Act adopts a progressive definition of disability which does allow for a considerably greater degree of coverage than the legislation currently proposed in the UK. At the same time, the fact that the Act is designed to cover a wide variety of situations makes it inevitable that some of its provisions can only be tested and clarified through the process of implementation. While this is perhaps a very positive function of progressive legislation, it does of course require efficient and equitable arbitration mechanisms in order to succeed.

Closely related to the need for appropriate arbitration and enforcement mechanisms is the need for information which would enable disabled people to exercise their rights effectively. As noted earlier, one of the potential limitations of purely legislative solutions to tackling discrimination is that some of the people who could benefit most from such measures are also those least likely to be able to exercise their rights. Consequently, as Marca Bristo points out in the context of implementing the Americans with Disabilities Act, once legislation is in place, it is equally important to ensure that people are informed of its existence and the rights and obligations which it entails. This not only enables disabled people to exercise their rights but, just as importantly, it enables employers, businesses and society in general to become more educated about why the legislation is required and what they need to do to make it work.

Potential wider benefits of removing disabling barriers

Finally, an important theme running through the various papers is that removing disabling barriers will involve developing universal solutions which go beyond the direct benefits to disabled people alone. The papers by Andrew Walker and Bryan Heiser, for example, provide persuasive arguments in favour of developing universal access which benefits society as a whole. Also, as Andrew Walker points out, this approach has much wider social benefits than simply making the environment more accessible for everyone; rather, developing universal access can also help to 'repair the split society of able-bodied and disabled people'. Similarly, Mike Oliver argues that removing the political, cultural and material barriers to participation faced by disabled people can help produce a more integrative and inclusive society for all.

The theme is echoed in several of the other chapters on specific types of disabling barrier. Len Barton, for example, argues that an inclusive education system which encompassed the needs of all would remove the need for special schools. Similarly, Caroline Gooding suggests that, if employment policies aimed to create opportunities for all workers, there would no longer be any need for quota schemes or similar measures to persuade employers to employ disabled people. Further, as Richard Berthoud's chapter illustrates, this would also reduce the need to compensate disabled people for the financial hardship created by their exclusion from the workforce.

Developing universal solutions to the removal of disabling barriers is clearly linked to the potential for broader political and cultural changes discussed earlier. However, some of the chapters also highlight that there can be much more immediate and practical benefits associated with enabling disabled people to make an active and positive contribution to the social and economic life of their communities. This, in turn, is closely linked to the ongoing debates about the costs of implementing anti-discrimination legislation. Although these costs are acknowledged, the various chapters that touch on this issue also highlight the substantial financial benefits which would follow from removing the barriers to disabled people's full participation in society. Further, while it is difficult to accurately quantify the level of these benefits in advance of implementing anti-discrimination legislation in this country, the evidence from the United States clearly suggests a potential for fairly speedy returns on whatever investment may be involved.

In conclusion, while there are obviously a number of issues still needing to be resolved, the evidence and arguments presented in this collection of papers also provide a clear indication of the potential for removing disabling barriers and the wider benefits which this would bring. Although anti-discrimination legislation on its own would not provide a complete solution to ending discrimination experienced by disabled people, it would nevertheless mark an important step towards enabling their full participation in society. By highlighting some of the key issues which need to be addressed, this publication will hopefully inform the development of appropriate policy solutions for ending discrimination and removing disabling barriers.

Part Two

The extent of discrimination and disadvantage

2 Disability, empowerment and the inclusive society

Mike Oliver

One of the things that concerns me is the way in which anti-discrimination and civil rights legislation has become the solution; not part of the solution to all the problems we, as disabled people, face; not a step on the road towards including disabled people into society, but the end of the road itself. I think we have to subject that assumption to critical analysis and that is one of the things I want to do in this chapter.

I took two books to read on holiday this summer. One was a book about the life and work of an Italian communist called Antonio Gramsci[1] who himself had an impairment (although he would not have identified himself as a disabled person in the way that those of us in the movement would talk about it today), and the other was the book by Lois Keith,[2] a collection of writings by disabled women.

For those who do not know about Gramsci, he was an Italian communist who was imprisoned by Mussolini and spent 15 years of his life in Mussolini's jails writing some very important social theory and writing it by hand in notebooks. I think for us the important message to come from Gramsci is in the key word 'hegemony', which is about the totality of experience. In order for people to understand what it is like to be disabled we have to understand the totality of that experience, and we have to resist attempts to divide up that experience, either in ways it has been done in the past by talking about the different experiences of different impairments – blindness, deafness, physical disability, learning difficulties and so on – or more recently, how it is increasingly being done in compartmentalising off bits of our lives and wanting to deal with them in little bits. The government proposes, for example, to attack discrimination in employment but leaves education and transport alone. We have to

17

begin to resist. What happens to us as disabled people happens in totality and it cannot be compartmentalised off and I think we need to remember that over the next few years as we get, as we inevitably will, civil rights legislation and as we continue our struggles for inclusion.

So, that is the first point that came out of my holiday reading. The second was a feeling of euphoria about how far we have come in our struggles, that we are nearly there; civil rights legislation is on the agenda, and it is certain that we will get it; therefore disabled people are going to get the kinds of thing that we deserve and are entitled to and disabled people will be included in the world in the future. Then I read the chapter by Merry Cross in Lois Keith's book and my euphoria was quickly dispelled. It should be essential reading for anyone who thinks that we are on the road to victory and that victory will come soon.

The chapter is about the abuse of disabled children, which increasingly, we are coming to learn, is a widespread problem. She cites two studies. One is a Canadian study which showed that 50 per cent of deaf children in residential schools in Canada experience physical or sexual abuse of one kind or another. The second is a study in this country; it shows that 98 per cent of young people with learning difficulties who were in residential accommodation experienced sexual abuse. Such figures are horrific and this is what she says about the abuse of disabled children:

> Perhaps it's the sheer depth of the pain and horror around abuse that prevents the disability movement from reaching first deep into the hearts of institutions for disabled people, youngsters and adults alike. For there at the centre of the oppression lie also the most abused of our number. There are the ones who are chosen because they cannot speak of the horror. There are the ones who are chosen because they cannot run away, and because there is nowhere to run. There are the ones who are chosen because their very lives depend upon not fighting back. There are the ones who are chosen because there is no-one for them to tell. There are the ones who are chosen because no-one has even taught them the words. There are the ones who are chosen because society chooses to believe that, after all, they don't really have any sexuality, so it can't hurt them.[3]

When we talk about progress, when we talk about anti-discrimination legislation, we need to bear in mind those groups. We need to address the issues, the ways in which society does the kind of oppressive and unspeakable things that it does to those vulnerable groups. And legislation is not the answer. It may be part of the answer but it is not *the* answer. There are many things that legislation cannot address.

Start, for example, with the way in which work is organised in the twentieth century. For the vast majority of time throughout the twentieth century, work has been organised around the twin principles of competition between individual workers and maximisation of profit. Inevitably disabled people have suffered because of the way work has been organised around those two principles; inevitably we have experienced exclusion from the workforce and even government commissioned research suggests that at least seven out of ten disabled people who are of working age do not have jobs.[4]

The only times that those figures have substantially changed have been during the two world wars. During the second world war, 430,000 disabled people who had previously been excluded from the workforce were incorporated into factories and into industry and not just in menial low grade tasks, but often doing important supervisory and managerial jobs.[5] The reason for that, it seems to me, is simple. The purpose of work during those two wars was not to maximise profit; the purpose was to fight the common enemy. Work was organised around the principles of cooperation and collaboration, not around the principles of competition and maximisation of profit.

At the end of the second world war, what we saw was the election of a government committed to ensuring that that situation continued and they passed legislation (and I think very important legislation) to ensure that disabled people were not excluded from the workforce. The reality is that, within three years, not only were most of those disabled people who had been included into the workforce out of jobs, but most of the other disabled people whose impairments had been created by the war, did not actually get into meaningful employment either. The old principles of the capitalist economy had reasserted themselves.

The legislation proved totally ineffective, not because, as many would argue, the legislation was bad, but simply because we live in a society which has a political culture which is based upon passing legislation which sets out broad philosophical principles and which then leaves it to gentlemen's agreements to make sure it is enforced. Now, that is all right if you are an eighteenth century landowner or a nineteenth century entrepreneur or even a twentieth century professional attending conferences like this. But if you are a member of one of the groups that Merry Cross talks about then you cannot expect legislation to solve the problems that you experience, or if you do, you will be sadly disappointed.

So while we want legislation, we must recognise the limits of that legislation. We must recognise that there are broader issues which are related to the way we organise work and the way our culture impacts, not just on disabled people's consciousness, but on everybody's consciousness. In the arena of culture, for example, disabled people experience exclusion. Disabled people are excluded from most of the main dominant forms of cultural dissemination and where we are included we are included in stereotypical fashion; we are villains or heroes, not ordinary people. We are made to conform to the stereotypes of disabled people as being emotionally stunted as well as physically impaired.

There is a substantial lack of disabled people participating at all levels within the main forms of cultural promotion and cultural dissemination. Of course one could suggest that a lot has happened over the last 15 years that offers grounds for optimism – and in some ways that is true. Disabled people in Britain are probably served better than anywhere else in the world in that we have a superb range of specialist disability programmes now. They have done a fine job over the last 15 years and we should recognise and acknowledge that. We have also had very good sensible coverage of the civil rights issue in recent months.

But these are, if you like, ripples on the pond – drops in the ocean. The reality still remains that as far as culture is concerned we are excluded; the main news programmes are still dominated by individualistic and tragic imagery, news stories about disability are usually about the latest search for the cure for some impairment or other, or trips for individual disabled children to Disneyland. Those are still the dominant kinds of story that you will read, see or hear about disabled people in the news media. And when do you see disabled people reading the news itself? We may be allowed to present our own programmes but when is somebody going to read *News at Ten* or chair *Question Time*?

If you look at other forms of cultural dissemination – films, television, books and so on – they are still dominated by the same old disabling and disablist imagery which presents us as pathetic, weak, tragic or indeed the opposite, heroic. Personally, I am fed up with being either a hero or some kind of pathetic victim of this appalling fate that others assume has befallen me.

Nor have we, in the twentieth century, been served very well by our political institutions. We cannot even get into most of them. From the House of Commons downwards it is virtually impossible to get in unless you make special arrangements and why the hell if we are political citizens should we have to make special arrangements; why should our political institutions make special arrangements to accommodate us? Certainly if any of us want to participate – though God knows why we might – in party politics at the local level, how many local constituency parties have accessible premises? For most of them you cannot even get into the bar, let alone any of the other areas. None of the political parties, again, I think have taken disability and disabled people's concerns seriously.

We have had lip service, we have had promises in manifestos before and no doubt we will get promises again. Personally I am not sure that I believe any of them. I remember – and this is just an example – a few years ago the Labour Party had heard the rhetoric of rights and it published its pamphlet about disability called *As of Right*. It used the kind of language we would use – the language of rights and how disabled people have rights – and it even demonstrated that it knew the difference between organisations of and for disabled people. However, at the end of the booklet it gave a list of useful addresses and every single organisation in that book was an organisation for the disabled, a non-democratic, non-accountable organisation. It did not give a single address of an organisation controlled and run by disabled people themselves. Its recent choice of a particular disabled person to the Social Justice Commission demonstrated that it has not learned much since.

We are also excluded from the process of politics in the sense that often we are expected to vote two or three days before anyone else if we want to use a postal vote. People with visual or sensory impairments do not get political information provided in the same way as everyone else. How many parties produce their manifestos in braille, for example? So in the twentieth century we have been excluded from the political system, from the political institutions and parties which are supposed to represent our views and our wishes and our needs, and from the political process in which our views are articulated.

Finally, in the twentieth century, one of the very institutions which was supposed to enable us and to include us – the welfare state – has served to exclude us. It has served to exclude us in a number of ways. It has served to exclude us through the provision and the continuing provision of residential institutions of all kinds, whether they be special schools, whether they be residential establishments, whether they be old people's homes, whether they be geriatric wards or whatever. We have been excluded through the construction and the continuation of a whole system of segregated residential institutions of one kind or another, and do not believe the rhetoric that the walls of the institutions are coming tumbling down. I have just seen recently the latest statistics on the integration of children with special needs into ordinary schools, only to find that more and more children are being segregated; that the minuscule trends towards integration that have occurred since the 1980s are now being reversed and we are actually segregating more children in the 1990s than we were in the 1980s.[6] *Parental choice ?*

There are other ways in which we are segregated as well. The benefits system itself serves to segregate. It serves to segregate people who are on benefits, it serves to create a dependency culture and – to use the language of the right – it serves to create an underclass. Those who argue that, as well as anti-discrimination legislation, the other solution to the problems that disabled people face is a national disability income would do well to reflect on the fact that one of the things that will happen if disabled people ever get a national disability income as a single one-off measure is that it will serve to legitimate the continued exclusion of disabled people from the workforce. So, we need to be very careful about proposals which offer single solutions to the hegemonic problems that we face. And finally, of course, the welfare state creates patronising attitudes towards us. The language which is used to talk about us still indicates that we are seen as passive and dependent people in need of care.

So, those are some of the barriers that we have faced in the twentieth century. What will civil rights legislation do about it? As I have already said, we have to recognise that civil rights legislation is a means to address some of these issues, it is not the solution to them. It is not the end, it is only the means and those of us who work in the movement need to be aware of the experience of the American movement in the 1970s. Having put a lot of energy into getting section 504 of the Rehabilitation Act and then forcing a recalcitrant administration and president eventually to sign it, the movement had nowhere to go. It experienced a downturn for a number of years because it had seen signing the legislation as being the end rather than the beginning. We are not going to make that mistake when we get civil rights legislation in this country – we are going to be prepared for the next stage of the struggle.

If we want to be included into twenty-first century society then we have to be prepared to recognise the extent and the totality of the oppression and discrimination that we face. Given the list and some of the things that I have gone through, I suppose it raises the question – is it possible for us to think that we can somehow successfully be included in the twenty-first century world? Well I am an optimist and I want to finish by giving a number of reasons as to why I am optimistic.

First, I am optimistic because work in the twenty-first century is changing. We šee evidence already that the nature of work is beginning to change. Again, to use sociological jargon, it is what sociologists refer to as post-Fordism: the idea that the organisation of work is changing, the way work is organised is changing. Often industries are finding it is more productive to organise work around principles of cooperation and collaboration rather than competition between wage labourers, and some industries are beginning to see that maximisation of profit is not the only or even the most important goal they should be pursuing.

So in the world of work we can see that there are grounds for optimism in that the nature and organisation of work may well change in the twenty-first century. That is not to say that we will not have to fight to be included, but nevertheless we have more of a chance of kicking the door open in the twenty-first century than we had in the twentieth century where, let us face it, it was economically rational not to take the risk of employing disabled workers amongst others, despite the rhetoric and despite the attempts that government and others have made over the years to pretend otherwise.

There is also evidence that we are beginning to make an impact in the cultural sphere. There is what some of us would call an emerging disability culture which you can see in the writings, the music, the paintings and the art that disabled people are producing for themselves but which you can also see in things like the guidelines that BCODP produce over media imagery.[7] You can also see it in the way that disabled people have refused to take lying down the kind of disablist rubbish that *Telethon* and *Children in Need* have been putting out and the very real victory that disabled people won by forcing the *Telethon* off of the air. Whatever else is said, do not let anyone ever tell you that the reason why *Telethon* disappeared was any other than the fact that the television companies were scared of what we might do the next time if they continued to put out such disabling garbage.

There is optimism about the political sphere too, not just because of the rise of our own movement, not just because of the way we have built local, national and international organisations controlled and run by us as disabled people, but also because the political institutions of the twentieth century are falling apart. We are actually talking now about republicanism, we are actually talking about the decline of the monarchy, we are actually talking about possible abolition which goes beyond Di and Charles and Squidgygate and all that. Royal families have always behaved in that kind of way and the public has always known that they have behaved in that kind of way. What is interesting in the late twentieth century is people saying, 'We are no longer prepared to put up with it, we are no longer prepared to pay for it.' So, there are questions being raised about the nature of the kind of democratic society in which we might live in the twenty-first century.

There are also fundamental questions that are going to be asked about the nature of democracy and whether democracy can be exercised through the political party system and just voting once every two years or every five years. Indeed one could say the party system is due to disappear because we do not have a party system any more. It is a bit like the good old USSR – there is only one party in Britain at present even though they have three different names. They have all got the same kind of policies and the opportunities for people to make meaningful choices about things that are of concern to them do not appear on their political agendas – whether that be concern about Europe or whether that be concern about personal violence and whether you can go outside your own front door. All the parties are broadly similar in terms of the kind of policies that they are talking about and, again, one of the things that the civil rights campaign demonstrated is that we do not have democratic institutions. When you have a country where it seems to me that the only people who were against civil rights legislation were John Major, Kenneth Clarke and a few people who play with the Treasury economic model on their computer, and everyone else was in favour of it, yet we still did not manage to get it, that raises fundamental questions about the nature of democracy. That is not just an issue for disabled people, that is an issue for all of us in terms of the kind of political institutions we have and the kind of society in which we live.

Finally, there is growing evidence that in the twenty-first century a new different kind of welfare state will emerge which will be based upon rights, entitlements and control. Again disabled people are in the forefront of struggles to create a different kind of welfare state which is not dominated by the needs of professionals and bureaucracies but where disabled people have created their own independent living schemes. At the end of the day, whether we like it or not, modern societies are not going to fund dependency-creating professionally-dominated welfare services in the twenty-first century.

The purpose of this publication, however, is to consider some of the more limited issues around anti-discrimination legislation and I want to finish by raising a number of issues on which we should focus. The first thing that we must remember is that when we get civil rights legislation – and we will – we are only going to get it once. Legislation in this country tends to go in 15-year cycles; governments pass legislation, they implement it, they monitor and they evaluate it, they then make decisions about whether it needs amending, scrapping, changing and so on and that normally takes about 15 years. It is normally a 15-year process – sometimes a bit shorter, sometimes a bit longer. If you look at disability, the last major legislation was 1970. Nothing else happened until 1986.

Once we get civil rights legislation we are going to be stuck with it for 15 years and therefore there are two important things we need to bear in mind. First, we need to get that legislation right. Second, we need to make sure it reaches into the lives of all disabled people; we need to make sure that it does not simply enable those of us that can and do, but also those people that Merry Cross talked about, to free themselves from the chains of oppression.

The final point that I want to make is that as disabled people we need to recognise that the law will not do it for us. Even once we have got legislation we will still have to do it ourselves. We will still have to force the politicians and the lawyers to take our concerns seriously. We will still have to go out on the streets. The road to liberation is one which we can only take for ourselves. But that should not be seen as an exclusionary or separatist argument. I hope that we will take – as Vic Finklestein calls them – people with abilities along with us.

References
1   P Ransome, *Antonio Gramsci: A New Introduction,* Harvester Wheatsheaf, 1992
2   L Keith (ed), *Mustn't Grumble,* Womens Press, 1994
3   M Cross in L Keith, 1994, pp.164-165

4   J Martin, A White and H Meltzer, *Disabled Adults: Services, Transport and Employment,* OPCS, 1988

5   S Humphreys and P Gordon, *Out of Sight: The Experience of Disability 1900-1950,* Northcote House Publishers, 1992

6   B Norwich, *Segregation and Inclusion: English LEA Statistics 1988-92,* Centre for Studies on Inclusive Education, 1994

7   C Barnes, *Disabling Imagery and the Media: An Exploration of the Principles for Media Representation of Disabled People,* Ryburn Publishing/BCODP, 1992

3 Segregated special education: some critical observations

Len Barton

In this chapter I will first examine some of the historical grounds for the introduction and maintenance of segregated schooling. Secondly, I will identify a series of criticisms of this form of provision including those by disabled people. Finally, I will highlight some of the current government policies as enshrined in the 1988 and 1993 Education Acts and their possible impact on the struggle for inclusive education.

Introduction

The question of segregated policy and provision in education is a complex and contentious issue. It is complex because an adequate understanding of the question involves a consideration of the relationship between political, economic and educational factors. It is contentious because of the degree to which people are committed to different and antagonistic values, priorities and visions of the type of society thought acceptable. This also includes the different perspectives on the social functions of education. Part of the difficulty relates to the degree to which individuals are passionate about their beliefs, even though they may be based on ignorance, misinformation and the fear of change.

Educational issues are contentious in that they involve struggles over meanings, acceptable practices and desirable outcomes. Thus the issues of grant-maintained schools, anti-racist educational policies, parental participation, single sex schools, and the national curriculum are all examples of highly contentious educational issues. They involve struggles between different interest groups motivated by alternative/ antagonistic beliefs and values. The question of segregated schooling is no exception. Passions often run very high whenever this topic is raised or reflected on in a critical manner as can be seen from the following statement by Cole, a principal of an independent boarding school for children with learning difficulties, whose book attempts to explore historically the role of integration in the policies and practices of special education. He maintains that:

> ... the rapid ending of all special schools, as proposed by the Children's Legal Centre for example, would be positively damaging to many children. To claim that integration is essentially a moral issue, and that to place a child in a separate special school usually denies him rights and damages his life chances, is unconvincing, often inaccurate and certainly insulting to the parents who support special schooling and to the many expert staff who have worked in the schools.[1]

What is vitally important is that the issue of segregation versus inclusive education is viewed not merely as being concerned with resources or different educational philosophies, but rather with fundamental values. It is about different conceptions of the good society, of images of self-identity and the relationship between education and society. Thus the demand for change is not solely educational; it is about the structural and social conditions of society itself. This type of relational thinking has motivated Hargreaves to maintain that teachers must be concerned with the social functions of schooling and therefore need to seriously engage with such questions as:

- What sort of society do we want to create or maintain?

- What is the role of education in creating or maintaining such a society?[2]

These are essential questions when a critical analysis of existing educational policies and practices is being constructed.

Historical grounds for segregated provision

Several reasons have been used as a justification for the establishment and maintenance of a system of segregated special provision. They include:

- Such schooling is essential in order to provide the *type* of education these children need.

- These children and young people need *protection* from the harsh and cruel realities of the world including those to be found in mainstream schools – their size, the attitudes of staff and pupils, verbal and physical abuse, etc.

- Special schools are staffed by teachers who have those necessary *qualities* of patience, dedication and love. Such schools provide good interpersonal relationships with staff.

- Special schools provide a special curriculum. One which is both *flexible* and *individualised* to meet the needs of pupils.

- Special schools prepare pupils to be as *normal-as-possible* and take their place in the post-school adult world.

- Special schools are necessary on *administrative efficiency grounds.* Thus, specialist teachers, equipment, support services are most effectively deployed.

What is vitally important to remember is that up to 1971 special schools were under the control of the Department of Health and Social Services. Many were known as Junior Training Centres. Now while the above reasons for such provision are depicted in positive terms and were influenced by humanitarian concerns, the dominant assumptions and perspectives influencing both policy and practice were medical and psychological.

This is reflected in the various categories that have been used to describe pupils attending special schools. These include 'subnormal', 'severely subnormal', 'delicate', 'maladjusted', 'mentally handicapped'. Stereotyping and stigmatisation resulted through the application of such negative labels. These as Apple argues have an 'essentialising' aspect to them, in that they tend to envelope an individual, highlighting their inabilities and unacceptable differences.[3] This has also been reinforced through the psychological ideas relating to intelligence and intelligence testing which have been influential in the construction of definitions including those of 'ability' and 'need'.

Several criticisms have been made of a range of aspects of special education. These include:

- Segregated provision tends to encourage negative labels, suspicion, stereotypes, fear and ignorance of a reciprocal nature.[4,5]

- Special schools are part of the disabling barriers within society and therefore need to be removed. This is a human rights issue.[6]

- Pupils within such schools receive an inferior education to their able-bodied peers and the rhetoric of 'caring' and 'supporting' often obscures this fact.[7]

- Such provision legitimates the notion of 'professional' as 'expert' and encourages passive dependency on the part of pupils.[8]

- Pupils suffer from low self-esteem significantly influenced by the low-expectations of staff with regard to the quality and extent of pupil learning.[9]

- The more the severity of the learning difficulty the greater the tendency to use didactic teaching approaches and the more controlling the forms of relationships.[10]

While we previously identified some of the positive grounds for the development of special schooling, these types of criticism provide the basis for a very different perspective. Thus it can be argued that special segregated provision is necessary in order to enhance the smooth running of mainstream schooling. The difficult, objectionable and unwanted pupils can be placed in these schools.

Special education from this perspective entails a discourse and practice of exclusion. It is socially restrictive. Set within the wider context of existing social conditions and relations, special education can be seen as an important means of social control. It is now society which needs to be protected and the social functions of such provision contributes to this requirement.

Voices of disabled people

Increasing numbers of disabled adults are reflecting back on their experience of being pupils in special schools. They are critical and are strongly advocating the closure of such schools.

This is Harriet reflecting on her experiences at a residential school for blind and partially blind girls:

> The most damaging thing was the way they destroyed your self-confidence. The way they said you couldn't do things because you were 'such and such' a person ... They really put you down ... I used to feel 'I'm nothing, I'm nobody, I can't do it'.[11]

The next statement is from Martin Yates who has cerebral palsy and is reflecting on his experience:

> In the 1970s when I went to school, special schools were the in thing. Everyone thought that was the best way of educating children with special needs.

> Special schools providing 'education'! Well that was a joke to start with, and as for being the better way I would not like to see any of the other

ways. Take it from a person who has been in a special school, there is very little, if any, education at all.[12]

Or, again, Jane Campbell illustrates the degree of her opposition to segregated provision:

> I am a whole hearted supporter and campaigner for the total integration of disabled children into mainstream schools and have been since the grand age of seven ... I hated the school bus because it took me away from my local friends, who were beginning to wonder why I didn't go to school with them. It also heightened my differences.[13]

Other disabled researchers, while not having been pupils in special schools, are also critical of them. In a discussion of able-bodied people's reaction to disability, Morris contends that:

> This is one of the most important lessons I have learnt. People's expectations of us are formed by their previous experience of disabled people. If disabled people are segregated, are treated as alien, as different in a fundamental way, then we will never be accepted as full members of society. This is the strongest argument against special schools and against separate provision.[14]

Or in a public lecture at the Irish Association of Teachers in Special Education, Oliver powerfully maintained that, with regard to the history of segregated provision, it has been:

> ... one of abject failure, whatever criteria we use to judge it ... Such has been the extent of this failure that nothing short of a complete destruction of the whole enterprise of special education will suffice to ensure that its reconstruction in the twenty first century will see the emergence of an enterprise that will be enabling, liberating and integrative for us all.[15]

One could multiply these examples as well as those criticisms expressed by organisations of disabled people nationally and internationally.

Inclusive provision

From these accounts it is possible to identify a series of benefits which inclusive education would provide. It would enable attendance at a local school which would foster friendships with local children and thereby remove ignorance and stereotypes. It would enable the pupils to experience the benefits of a broad curriculum, access to more teachers and greater opportunities to develop self esteem and confidence.[16] Through this means an alternative would be developed to the mystique and expert dependency ethos of special schooling.

Inclusive education is concerned with the well being of *all* pupils and schools should be welcoming institutions. Inclusive policy and practice needs to be part of a whole-school policy and entails several important principles including those listed below:

Some principles underpinning whole-school policies

- Disability is an equal opportunities issue.

- The aims of education are the same for all children.

- The curriculum must take into account the changing society in which we live.

- All teachers who are 'specialists' in 'special educational needs' are teachers of all children.

- All children are entitled to equal opportunities to study all subjects that the school offers.

- Any form of discrimination or segregation is to be avoided; intervention should take place in as normal a setting as possible.

- Parental and community involvement is essential.[17]

It is essential that the demand for inclusive education does not result in a critique of special schooling which becomes an end in itself. We are also advocating that these developments cannot adequately be achieved in terms of the existing conditions and relations in mainstream schools. They too will need to change and there are certain features that are unacceptable, including the plant, organisation, ethos, pedagogy and curriculum. It will demand the transfer of resources, careful planning and continual monitoring. We are not advocating a dumping practice into existing provision.

One of the contributory factors to the failing of past attempts to seriously challenge segregated provision has been the lack of political will on the part of the government. Current government policies in relation to education need to be carefully considered, particularly as there are growing signs of an increase in disabling barriers thereby undermining the campaign for inclusive education.

Market ideologies and education

Successive Conservative governments have introduced a series of major policy changes in education which have covered all aspects of practice including, finance, governing bodies, curriculum, assessment, opting out, nursery education and teacher training. Such changes have been informed by a market ideology in which the goals of education and how to achieve them are being significantly shaped by market forces.

Market forces are alleged to be an efficient means of creating the conditions and relationships necessary for freedom of consumers, for allocating scarce resources, generating diversity and providing the form of flexibility the new order requires. The market has thus both economic and social functions.[18] This has been largely achieved through a populist discourse in which diversity and choice have been the key components. The role of legislation has been of major importance in the reconstruction of educational provision and practice. Schools have been depicted as failing in the area of standards and discipline, thereby contributing to our inabilities as a nation to be competitive in the international market place. Under the guise of reducing state control the role and powers of LEAs have been radically reduced, local management of schools has been introduced and the working conditions and definition of teachers' work has been changed. A new form of language has been introduced by which we both think about and evaluate education – it is the language of business. Thus, 'quality', 'accountability', 'cost-efficiency', 'effectiveness', 'performance-indicators', 'development plans', 'mission statements', 'targets', and 'appraisal' are key concepts in this discourse.

Through diversity of provision and a strong emphasis on competitiveness schools are encouraged increasingly to be concerned with presentation management skills and the necessity of selling themselves or suffering the consequences. Opting-out into grant-maintained status, being successful in the published league tables of examination results and having low truancy rates are all incentives to increase their status and economic position. Aggressive promotion drives through, for example, the introduction of new brochures and school uniforms created through the appointment or service of public relations and design personnel, are now a feature of increasing numbers of schools.

Conservative governments have evidenced their antagonism to comprehensive education by the introduction of a diversified and hierarchical system of provision. We now have grammar schools, grant-maintained schools, city technology schools, secondary modern schools and technology schools.[19]

In such a system of provision, status and stigmatisation will be exacerbated through a sharper dichotomy between successful and so called 'sink-schools'. The possibility of selective practices taking place both in terms of access to particular schools and opportunities within them are increasing.[20] In this climate, the pursuit of inclusive education becomes highly problematic. For example, we now know from English LEA statistics for 5 to 15 year olds that:

> From 1991-92 there was a small national increase in special school placements across English LEAs, contrasting with the past decade's gradual trend towards more inclusive education.

and

> In January 1992, the special school population went up to 88, 952 pupils, or from 1.47% in 1991 to 1.49% of all 5-15 year old pupils.[21]

Wide variation with regard to LEA placements of disabled children is still a marked feature of the current situation.

More alarming was the announcement in August 1994 of the first grant-maintained special school – Whitefield Schools and Centre, Waltham Forest. This was because from 1 April 1994 special schools were given the opportunity to opt out. While official documents may be used to suggest government support for so-called integration in the light of the above development, they seem to be examples of empty rhetoric. This is best demonstrated in the statement given by the education minister, Eric Forth, when he announced the approval of grant-maintained status for Whitefield Schools and Centre. He said:

> I hope that other special schools will follow Whitefield's example and look forward to welcoming more special schools into the growing GM sector.[22]

The fact that this policy has been less successful than the government had hoped with regard to mainstream schools does not seem to have deterred them from seeking support from the special school sector. What is worrying from the perspective adopted in this chapter is that here we have a clear government sponsorship and legitimation of segregated provision and practice.

Even in relation to integration practices within mainstream schools there is evidence of serious difficulties beginning to emerge. This can be seen from the following warning made by a group of researchers examining the impact of the market on comprehensive schools:

> ... there may be longer-term costs involved in giving too high a profile to SEN work; market image, national testing performance and staying-on rates in the sixth form may conspire to produce new kinds of exclusion or marginalisation for SEN students. Schools will face ethical dilemmas which set professionals' commitments against financial expediency.[23]

In an article on the new changes to the law relating to exclusions within schools Taylor, a headteacher of South Manchester High School, highlights some of what he maintains are the damaging effects of government policy:

> Exclusion has always been a controversial issue, and in the free market jungle which the government has introduced and fostered, it will cause increasing problems, whatever the law says. When one considers how many support services – educational psychologists, social workers, education welfare officers, advisory teachers, child guidance centres, child psychiatrists – have been decimated as a direct result of government funding policies, one is forced to conclude that responsibility for the current rate of exclusions does not rest with schools. Nor will they be to blame for the explosion to come.[24]

This has serious implications for all children in our maintained schools and particularly those schools who are striving to adopt and implement whole-school inclusive policies.

These developments raise some serious questions. For example:

- How far will market-led decision making in education lead to an increase in segregated provision?

- Will the pupil make-up within such schools be overly representative of children from particular socio-economic and racial backgrounds?

- Within a period of such intensive and rapid reconstruction, how far will teachers be able and/or willing to express a strong commitment to the entitlement and rights of disabled children?

- How far will these changes influence the development of a negative view of difference?

Full inclusion in society is a matter of profound concern. It is a human rights issue involving participation, choice and empowerment. Issues of social justice and equity are central to the demands for inclusive education. There is no room for complacency. This is a serious struggle. The notion of 'struggle' reflects the stubbornness of structural and social barriers which have to be overcome as well as the level of commitment required by those of us engaged in this task.

Equal opportunities policy

Inclusive education needs to be part of a whole-school equal opportunities policy. If we are to resist complacency and recognise the degree of struggle still to be engaged with, and if official rhetoric is to be translated into reality in substantive terms in the lives of *all* citizens, then the question of inclusive education needs to be an integral part of a well thought through, adequately resourced and carefully monitored equal opportunities policy. By being an integral part of an equal opportunities approach it will provide a basis for the identification of those features of the existing society including, policy and practices within specific institutions and contexts, that are offensive, unacceptable and thus must be challenged and changed.

What this chapter is advocating therefore is that making a difference within schools must be explicitly recast in broader social, political and moral terms.[25]

Conclusion

The transition from segregated special schools to inclusive provision and practice will demand careful planning and sensitive implementation. In the current context some parents prefer their children to attend a special day or residential school. From the perspective adopted in this chapter such choices should not be viewed as a defence for the continuation of special schools, but rather, as Dessent has forcefully argued:

> Special schools do not have a right to exist. *They exist because of the limitations of ordinary schools in providing for the full range of abilities and disabilities amongst children.* It is not primarily a question of the quality or adequacy of what is offered in a special school. Even a superbly well organised special school offering the highest quality curriculum and educational input to its children has no right to exist if that same education can be provided in a mainstream school.[26] [my emphasis]

Such provision needs to be struggled for in order that institutional discrimination in the form of segregated special schooling is ameliorated. Current educational policies, resulting in a diversified and hierarchical form of schooling, are making this task much more difficult.

References
1   T Cole, *Apart or A Part: Integration and the Growth of British Special Education*, Open University Press, 1989
2   D Hargreaves, *Challenge to the Comprehensive School*, Routledge and Kegan Paul, 1982, p.85
3   M Apple, *Ideology and Curriculum*, Routledge and Kegan Paul, 1990
4   C Barnes, *Disabled People in Britain and Discrimination: A Case for Anti-Discrimination Legislation*, Hurst and Company, 1991
5   R Rieser and M Mason, (eds), *Disability Equality in the Classroom: A Human Rights Issue*, ILEA, 1990

6   M Oliver, 'Does Special Education have a Role to Play in the Twenty F
    Century', Paper given at the Irish Association of Teachers in Special Education
    6th Annual Conference, 1994

7   M Oliver, 'Intellectual Masturbation: A rejoinder to Soder and Booth',
    European Journal of Special Needs Education, vol.7, no.1, 1992, pp.20-28
    S Tomlinson, *A Sociology of Special Education*, Routledge and Kegan Paul,
    1982

9   A Freeman and H Gray, *Organising Special Educational Needs: A Critical
    Approach*, Paul Chapman, 1989

10 A Brechin and J Swain, 'Professional/Client Relationships: Creating a "working
    alliance" with people with learning difficulties', *Disability, Handicap and
    Society*, vol.3, no.3, 1988, pp.213-226

11 Quoted in S French, 'Out of Sight, Out of Mind: The Experience and Effects
    of a "Special" Residential School', (unpublished paper), 1994

12 M Yates, 'The Special School Survivor,' *New Learning Together*, 1, 1994,
    pp.42-43

13 J Campbell, 'Ex-Pupil's Account' in R Rieser and M Mason (eds), *Disability
    Equality in the Classroom: A Human Rights Issue*, ILEA, 1990, p.168

14 J Morris, 'Progress with Humanity. The experience of a disabled lecturer',
    in R Rieser and M Mason (eds), *Disability Equality in the Classroom: A
    Human Rights Issue*, ILEA, 1990, p.59

15 M Oliver, 'Does Special Education have a Role to Play in the Twenty First
    Century', Paper given at the Irish Association of Teachers in Special Education,
    6th Annual Conference, 1994

16 A Freeman and H Gray, *Organising Special Educational Needs: A Critical
    Approach*, Paul Chapman, 1989

17 A Freeman and H Gray (as above)

18 S Ranson 'Markets or democracy for education', *British Journal of Educational
    Studies*, vol.41, no.4, 1993, pp.333-352

19 B Simon and C Chitty, *SOS. Save Our Schools*, Lawrence and Wishart, 1993

20 G Walford, 'Selection for Secondary Schooling', National Commission on
    Education, Briefing Paper No.7, 1992

21 B Norwich, *Segregation and Inclusion, English LEA Statistics 1988-92*, CSIE,
    1994

22 E Forth, *DFE News*, No.209/94, DFE, 1994

23 R Bowe, S Ball and A Gold, *Reforming Education and Changing Schools:
    Case Studies in Policy Sociology*, Routledge and Kegan Paul, 1992, p.137

24 P Taylor, 'No possibilities can be excluded', *Times Educational Supplement*,
    16 September 1994, p.20

25 M Fullan, *Change Forces. Probing the Depths of Educational Reform*, Falmer
    Press, 1993

26 T Dessent, *Making the Ordinary School Special*, Falmer Press, 1987, p.97

4   Universal access and the built environment – or from glacier to garden gate

Andrew Walker

I have called this talk 'from glacier to garden gate'. In order to remain in equilibrium all parts of any structure must be able to move one with the other in a balanced way. Otherwise chaos and collapse occur. If we wish to live in a harmonious environment then it is essential to make an integrated appraisal of the whole picture. Unwittingly, our professions are tending to take too narrow a perspective on their own roles. This does not have a healthy effect upon our environment, culture or economy.

The minority of those involved in the world of design who tend to be male and in their thirties do not design for the world about them; but only the world they see. The needs of the majority – their parents, grandparents and children, their girlfriends – are not embraced. They have created a disabling environment for all people. What is needed to be addressed is the very positive and exciting concept – that of a universally accessible environment.

In order to put this in context and to try to take you beyond the world of building regulations, I would like to share a recent experience I had when recently visiting another European country one night for a conference.

I booked my flight in the usual way at my travel agency and returned to the office. Two hours later I received a telephone call to say that, as a wheelchair user, I would not be allowed to travel alone on that airline. I was astonished at this. I thought that we are now one big union of states with freedom to travel – indeed commute – between London and other capitals. These things I naively believed were being fostered by the European Union. I have travelled to many countries alone on long and short haul flights without encountering this form of blatant discrimination before.

regulations to prevent plagues. Little wonder that a culture came about putting disabled people in the middle of this. Some outside force is required to persuade the bureaucracies to rethink the philosophy that disabled people are disease-spreading arsonists. We need as strong an intellectual and political commitment as that which established the regulations in the first place in order to remove the misplaced use of regulation. The 1667 Act did not beat about the bush by demanding four sorts of building and no more. It led to the finest town planning of any city in the world and also the most flexible form of building construction in the London terrace house. There were penalties for non-compliance. No talk of persuasion at all. Plenty of scope and wondrous inventive detail. Of course mistakes were made, as they can expect to be, but the point is they were bold, imaginative and not afraid.

The airline culture can adopt the notion of universal access with greater ease than our regulatory bodies on the ground. It carries much less baggage. But access needs on the ground are the same as in the sky – a combination of decent design and sensible management. They embrace all people, not just people with disabilities, but also people who one would think of as non-disabled but, in common with us, are disabled by the environment. Compulsory inaccessibility is like compulsory celibacy, without joy. We need choices in order to flourish. The built environment can be extremely important in promoting access and choice. It can help provide the physical connections to repair the split society of able-bodied and disabled people. Planners, architects, building control officers, licensing officers (note 'officers' in our best militaristic tradition), judges, cinema managers and so on, are often seen as gaolers by us. Disabled people appear to non-disabled people as objects, nuisances, and costly items of unnecessary expenditure. Interdependence one with the other is a necessity where design and disability are concerned.

The old patronising attitude of the professions to disabled people has to go. This means we need confidence in those who create our environment. We do not have it. If the fear between us is to be diminished the professions need to woo the disability movement. Despite probably the best intentions, matters have been made worse by the creation of what I must call a Special Needs Industry, reinforcing the idea that disabled people require the charity of the general public as though not part of it. Part M (of the Building Regulations) itself has given us all a good deal to think about and improved life for many of us. But it has reinforced the idea that people with disabilities have very special demands. It was important to highlight the issue when it was introduced, but the government should now take an important step: integrate, not separate. Part M still does not embrace any minimally accessible housing standard and has not grasped the nettle of material alterations or retrofit. We enjoy making life difficult for ourselves. I do not think the nettle can be grasped in the absence of an overall policy. Society rightly expects reasons and should be given a policy. Access is still not part of the culture – public money is still invested in poorly accessible national buildings and the architects are not penalised. Any architect seeking advice visits the Access Officer *for The Disabled* not just an access adviser. Government reinforces the notion giving Department of Health, not Environment, funding to the Centre for Accessible Environments and the Access Committee for England, both bodies dealing with environmental issues.

In order to function in daily life everyone has access needs. But we must keep a sense of perspective and toleration. Some people have more elaborate needs than most. A few examples can be cited. Politicians need limousines, control of the media, armed forces and protection; the aristocracy need palaces, processions, regalia, carriages and, of course, good causes; the clergy need congregations, cathedrals, vestments and icons. The financial cost to society is not at all small for these access needs. You would find it extraordinary if I were to refer to these people without these necessities for their survival as 'invalid' wouldn't you?

Yet the only thing people with disabilities ask is sensitive design, sometimes necessarily linked to careful management. Is this too much to ask? Can this really be termed a 'special' need? I think you will agree that, compared with the extraordinary demands of certain sections of the population it is positively mundane.

Matthew Parris in the *Times* of 16 May 1994 writes that 'the disabled are unwise to chip away at what will always be the surest foundation for their argument: the good will of the able-bodied'. So now you have it – the greatest special need of all lies not with people with disabilities but with the right of expectancy of non-disabled people themselves!

Of course there are very serious questions and needs for certain sections of the population. But where costs are concerned we must stress the positive aspects and try to see things from different perspectives. We expect Parliament to do so too. Five years ago we were told there was no discrimination. Now we are too expensive. I believe that only once before in our history has the cost tag been put on human rights. This was when the first attempts were made to abolish the slave trade. Beware – the curmudgeons have resurfaced.

When Parliament voted for Civil Rights, the government suddenly produced the figure of £17 billion, with the environment provisions constituting the main part at £10 billion. The first sentence of the evidence admits that the figures are not to be relied upon. A new meaning indeed to 'publish and be damned'. In addition to admitted inaccuracies the other half of the equation, the costs of inaccessibility, was ignored. Swift replies from the Access Committee for England and the Rights Now Campaign have put the boot into the figures – double-accounting, twice estimating the cost of access provision, over-estimating the size of the private sector and the lack of cost-benefit analysis – but have been ignored by the mainstream and industrial press. Where is the cost of altering publicly funded new buildings mentioned? The list is as long as time permits, whether it is art galleries from Cornwall to Yorkshire or, in London, the latest cinema, museum or passenger terminal. This is not retrofit, but attempting to correct current modern design. Redress is needed. What price the cost of adapting houses to suit the majority of the population? The government boasts about the increases in the amount it spends on having to adapt houses. How much of this money need be spent if the design were not archaic? What is the cost to industry of preventing people from buying goods, clothes, going on holidays, visiting the cinema, night clubs, bars, bookshops, historic buildings or simply getting a job? What is the cost to our culture in having so few people with disabilities in the professions that set the standards and create the buildings? And we are the only country which still uses money and has discovered disabled people? If not, where are the comparative studies?

Now to the government's consultation document, *Measures to Tackle Discrimination against Disabled People*. Previously there have been attempts to 'target' certain sections of the population. This does not appear to have met with a great deal of success. The poor are still very poor. Now this document has the idea of 'key' areas, a somewhat similar approach, but the scope is very limited. What is the point of:

> Item (16) discrimination would be outlawed in a variety of areas including access to public places ... exceptions to this rule would include: ... where existing physical barriers prevent access.[1]

Throughout the piece on the Building Regulations the disadvantages are emphasised.

> For example, the extra cost for home buyers or the restrictions on design freedom which some of these proposals would produce cannot be ignored.[2]

The same negative thoughts are not erected where foundations, plumbing or insulation are concerned. Obviously the author knows little about how designers or architects work or think. Then the document gets on to garden gates. Of course houses should be accessible except where geographically impossible. It is not a problem. It is not more costly. I must say when I first caught sight of the document I could not remember when I last saw a garden gate. There is nothing in the world stopping anyone changing their garden gate if they do not like it. Do you really imagine the Access Officer is going to rush round demanding to know why you have changed your garden gate? Garden gates are like front doors: they need to be wide enough to let a pram, a wheelchair and a coffin through. In that order.

Do you see what I am getting at when I refer to detail? A friend returned from Alaska after her summer holiday. 'It's amazing', she said. 'We've had a wonderful time. They've even got accessible glaciers!' That is what I mean by scope.

I do not understand why the proposal is so limited. It is necessary to take a global view of discrimination; otherwise the proposal has no integrity and there is nothing to which the separate parts can relate. A policy acceptable to disabled people cannot be formed on this basis. Is it necessary to be so parochial? It would have been helpful if there had been an attempt to explain what is happening elsewhere; to inform our response and remove some fears. Nowhere is any comparison with standards in other members of the EU, the Commonwealth or the United States made. Perhaps the research is not available. It should be. I am informed that there is a proposal before the Disability Sub-Committee in Greenwich Council to work as though the Bill is active – so much is a framework needed.

The issues are not new. The talk about revising mobility standard housing, for example, and producing something which could be applied across the board has been discussed for at least a decade. Two issues have arisen: how to house severely disabled people and how to build houses which will be of much more use to the general public as occupants age. Both the Access Committee for England (ACE) and the Joseph Rowntree Foundation have produced their standards.

The difference between them is of interest. The ACE standard has evolved in a climate which relates to the desire to include housing within Part M of the Building Regulations and enable new housing to be accessible to all people, but not a wheelchair housing standard. The emphasis has been on the saving of expenditure in the long term and the formulation of a standard that, like the earlier mobility one, would provide housing at no or negligible increase in cost. It would make an enormous difference and put an end to the business of elderly people having to purchase quite costly inaccessible retirement homes which they then find they shortly have to move away from because they just cannot move around in them or enter or leave them without help. Its standard in houses which would already be designed to have a ground floor lavatory would cost only £350 more.[3] The ACE standard is not a space but an access standard, and should be a minimum requirement for general accessible housing throughout the private sector and that advocated for the extension to Part M.

The new standard produced by the Joseph Rowntree Foundation is that of Lifetime Homes and is designed for a family which can include a wheelchair user. This incorporates turning circles in planning the ground floor rooms, including the ground floor lavatory which could become a shower. In the upper floor it would be possible to move from bedroom to bathroom using a hoist. A stairlift or a house lift could easily be added. Parking spaces are slightly more generous than those of ACE.

The two standards have a common philosophy relating to the approach and entrance, with level platform at the external doors. Both have common external and internal door widths and corridor widths and insist on a ground floor lavatory. They are interesting in that they refer to houses and flats and not merely 'bungalow' planning. There is no reason to believe that disabled people like to spend their life on the ground floor with no aspect other than a low sill in the sitting room. The reality of urban settings and the desire for integration are both being confronted.

The Lifetime Homes standard does cost more. Actual examples are the costings for houses built at Foxwood, a suburb of York. The cost of land and the costs of building in, say, the south of England or in the centres of towns would probably be greater.

*The total additional costs are £484 for a 1 bedroom flat of 5 0.6m²
and £747 for a 2 bedroom house of 73.2m².*

1 Bedroom, 2 Person Flat (50.6m²)	Additional cost per dwelling
Stairs	124
Adjustments to external walls windows etc	297
Adjustments to internal partitions, doors etc	63

2 Bedroom, 4 Person House (73,2m²)	Additional cost per dwelling
Stairs	248
Adjustments to internal partitions, doors etc	26
Additional w.c. downstairs	408
Strengthening first floor bathroom partition walls	6

Source: JRF standards report[4]

In a recent study undertaken by the RIBA the political policies
of the major political parties were examined; none had taken on board
the issue of accessible housing. Everyone agrees some legislation is
required. Almost a quarter of a century ago the Chronically Sick and
Disabled Persons Act was introduced and later modified. It could have
been the model for anti-discrimination legislation. But it was never
fully implemented. Whereas the shiny new American model in the
Americans with Disabilities Act (note the Americans are not
Handicapped now but have Disabilities) has teeth and claws. Indeed,
because of the disabling nature of their products, if the Americans
with Disabilities Act were to be applied across the countries of the
European Union every single state would contain architectural practices
faced with court injunctions and liable to fines – echoes of our 1667
Act – of up to the equivalent of $100,000. Such a threat here would
work wonders in exorcising the religion of steps from the architectural
psyche.

As architects we are capable of meeting society's demands and
have consequently become experts in the architecture of separation.
Now it is necessary to develop the art of the wider perspective which
includes all people. This will create new forms of architecture and is
seen already to be happening in some of our public buildings. But
to meet this challenge successfully architects must be prepared to

learn from the people for whom they have been creating a disabling environment – the real experts who know about access needs.

Work undertaken by Milner and Urquhart from Robert Gordon's Institute of Technology, Aberdeen, on the prevalence of the access issue in architectural schools tells us:

> Only eight have course documentation which specifically refers to the access requirements of disabled people. Overall, the approach adopted is piecemeal, inconsistent and largely discretionary. Until such times the syllabus content within architectural education incorporates universal design as a requirement, there will remain a lack of incentive to adopt and apply the concept, with a continuing functional failure of public buildings in particular.[5]

It will generally not be taught as universal access, but for a group who have some sort of disability. Similarly, dissatisfaction with the way in which the access issue is being taught, or ignored, led to the creation in my own school of a day-release, multi-disciplinary post-graduate diploma in Environmental Access. The aim of the course is to bring together various disciplines to promote a less hostile environment in terms of architecture and design as, like architecture itself, the Access Issue is not the confine of one profession. Integrated with this aim, people who are directly affected by a disabling environment are naturally included, as students, educators, and innovators.

The presence of the experts, of people with disabilities, has been a positive one. An induction course is a compulsory preliminary element for our post-graduate students. We have introduced access into the undergraduate school in terms of perceptions of space. The students are taught by disabled people. Also each of our post-graduate students will be linked with architectural or other practices.

All design students should be aware of the need to promote universal access and that within it is embodied the more particular requirements of people with a disability. Both areas can be pursued as a specialism and both require a sound aesthetic base.

I do not say disabled people have all the answers. The advice needs to come from a balanced group. Disabled people are at the source of the issue. But I can tell you of a major project where naive architects, of international fame, took ill considered advice from a wheelchair user and the result is a building without the universal access the client demanded. And it will be the architects who get the bad press.

It is not possible to know where the attempt to create a universally accessible environment may lead. Some elements already exist. For example it is accepted that there is no longer someone to open the door for you. The technology allowing doors to open as one approaches and conveniently close behind, keeping in the heat, is now a necessity. Some things may disappear from the culture – the hierarchial architectural design with flights of steps will be replaced with access on the level; the architectural apartheid of the revolving doors for some people, with the side door for disabled people and service, replaced by a single entrance; easily climbable stairs; reception areas where everyone can be properly received; easily understood graphics; lifts to all areas; lavatories with all doors opening outwards; high and low washbasins; unsegregated areas in lavatories, restaurants, bars, clubs, hotels. An end to the architecture of monochrome, exquisitely unusable sculptural forms. Houses which can be used by all people and are thought of as long term habitations and not only commodities. The development of a real feel for the movement of people through spaces and the connection between outside and inside. A greater awareness of the perceptions of space relating to people's need for sound, vision and communication. And beyond architecture there would be, for example, level access to trains and buses and spaces for wheelchair users on aircraft. A broad scope in which technology, invention and art would have a great deal of play. Many of these notions are ancient but need re-stating.

The first move towards the creation of such an environment must be the introduction of fully comprehensive civil rights legislation. The approach must be positive and bold; not benevolent and embarrassed. Cultural change can only come about by the use of law and education. Then the labels we stick on ourselves – 'disabled' and 'able bodied' – may no longer be needed.

References
1   DSS Disability Unit, *Consultation on Government Measures to Tackle Discrimination Against Disabled People,* HMSO, 1994
2   Ibid.
3   S Aaronovitch, *Accessible Housing: What does it cost?,* Access Committee for England, December 1993
4   JRF *Lifetime Homes Study,* Joseph Rowntree Foundation, 1992
5   R Milner and J Urquhart, *Access by Design,* 56, 1991

5 The nature and causes of transport disability in Britain, and how to remove it

Bryan Heiser

What is transport disability?

I understand disability to be a particular form of oppression which arises when impaired people are unreasonably excluded from any social right or social good, and transport disability to be the unnecessary exclusion of disabled people from current forms of transport, especially public transport. By public transport I mean buses, trains, and all subsidised and publicly organised transport and I take in to some extent taxis and hire cars and other modes that may be brought into the public transport arena. I start from the principle that nobody should or need be excluded from public transport.

Two illustrations summarise this: examples of the reality that exists in different places in different countries. In the illustrations I am using wheelchair use as symbolising or summarising the whole range of impairments which public transport in this country does not accommodate, or accommodates unsatisfactorily, putting the individual at a disadvantage compared to most users. I intend the idea of a wheelchair to be an inclusive symbol.

The first illustration shows somebody using a wheelchair getting off a bus which has completely flat access, without assistance (Figure 1).[1] The second shows somebody getting a buggy on to the bus, also unaided: because the access is flat there is no problem (Figure 2). Of course I cannot vouch for what is inside the bus: we cannot see that; but the illustration is intended simply to make the point that what I conceive as an ideal transport system can exist. We have the technology, we have the knowhow.

The ideal transport system as I imagine it is a mix of accessible equipment – the vehicles, the stations, the platforms, the bus stops – and ways of operating that do not create barriers to universal use. I

Figure 1

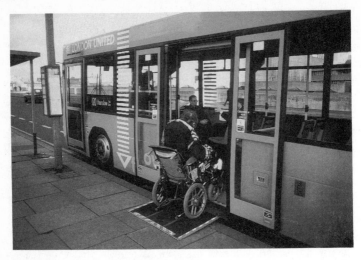

believe that there is no reason why all buses and trains should not be accessible to everyone.

Without trying to list every feature they would need, some obvious ones are: flat, ramped or lift access, grab rails, comfortable seats, audio information, written information, helpful conductors and toilets where appropriate. The way the transport is operated will require a

Figure 2

combination of buses deviating from routes, some buses bookable and door to door, subsidised use of taxis and mini cabs, subsidised arrangements for individuals' own vehicles and drivers. A public transport system that includes these features – and more – will allow all people to use it with safety, confidence and dignity.

The reality in Britain in the 1990s is illustrated by the sort of physical problem we are confronted with every day: steps up to buses, steps inside the buses, narrow gangways, unfriendly seats, no help in the bus, no good visual or audio information, bus stops not having any kind of raised loading quays, no seats, no shelters, trains that are inaccessible, inaccessible toilets. I imagine that we all know what public transport is like in this country and that those of us who diverge significantly from a stereotype of ideal humanity find it difficult or impossible to use.

Some of the difficulties which perhaps are not frequently thought about are to do with operating regimes. Perhaps many of us take for granted that public transport should run only according to schedules and fixed routes; that the scheduling is tight; that people have little time to get on and off; that individual passengers have to conform to the schedule rather than vice versa.

And there are economic issues as well: those existing forms of transport which are more helpful to a wide range of people – for example taxis, minicabs and hire cars – are the very ones that are most expensive and tend not to be subsidised. And this is in a situation where disabled people have less resources than others, not more. While we have what are defined as special needs (defined as special needs simply because of the way transport is constructed and operated) no financial advantage accrues to anyone between the levels of the state and the individual, broadly speaking, in meeting those needs.

The number of transport disabled people in Britain

For a first approach to estimating the number of transport disabled people it is helpful to consider the average number of journeys made each year by different types of transport per person in the UK. Table 1 gives this information for 1991-93.

Overwhelmingly most journeys per person are made by car – as drivers or passengers. We know that disabled people, who are older and poorer than the general population, tend to have less access to cars, and have fewer cars in the family.

The next most frequent mode of transport is walking; it is obvious that walking is one of the things which many disabled people find rather problematic.

The next two most frequently used forms of transport are local buses and London Underground (which latter I have boosted roughly pro rata to give a national figure). Given the obvious inaccessibility of these types of transport this represents an additional 117 trips per person per year which many disabled people are excluded from. And so on.

Table 1   Number of journeys made per person, UK, 1991-93

Mode of travel	Number of journeys made each year per person (UK)
car (driver / passenger)	616
walking[*]	310
local bus	67
London underground	(50) pro-rata
bicycle	19
train	11
taxi/minicab	10
motorcycle	5
other[**]	1

[*]   as defined in the survey

[**]   includes air travel and non-BR rail, dial-a-rides and other forms of accessible special transport

Source: National Travel Survey 1991-93 [2]

This table demonstrates that most of the journeys that people make in this country are journeys which disabled people find problematical or impossible. The bottom row – 'other' – is a rag bag where of course we find disabled people: Dial-a-Rides and other forms of accessible special transport are in there. All 'other' types of journey add up to less than one journey per person per year. Given the number of disabled people in Britain that bottom row should have a figure more like 16 if the number of journeys we made by 'other' transport was proportionate to the number made by the rest of the population (this estimate does not acknowledge the journeys disabled people make by conventional transport).

Table 2   Characteristics of impairment in our society

About -

- 4.3 million people cannot walk 1/4 mile without stopping and without severe discomfort
- 3 million people cannot walk 200 yards without stopping and without severe discomfort
- 2.3 million people cannot stand for 10 minutes without severe discomfort
- 1.7 million people cannot stand for 5 minutes without severe discomfort
- 0.5 million people cannot walk up or down one step unaided
- 1 million people need all the time to hold on to something to keep their balance
- 1 million people need quite often to hold on to something to keep their balance
- 200,000 people cannot see a person standing on the other side of the road
- 300,000 people cannot see well enough to read a newspaper headline
- 1 million people have difficulty hearing someone talking at normal volume in a quiet room
- 1 million people have great difficulty following a conversation if there is background noise
- 0.5 million people lose control of their bladder at least daily
- 200,000 people are understood with difficulty by others
- 0.5 million people have difficulty understanding what other people are saying

Source: OPCS Disability Surveys[3]

A second approach to estimating the number of transport-disabled people considers the prevalence of different common impairments. This approach involves considering the characteristics of people in this country in terms of what you need to be able to do to use public transport. Table 2 sets out the numbers of people who cannot do some of the things that currently organised public transport requires.

For example, if you cannot walk a quarter of a mile without stopping and without severe discomfort – which may mean you simply cannot use a local bus service – you are not alone: there are nearly

4.3 million other people like you. And so on down the list, which suggests the numbers of people with physical, sensory and intellectual impairments who are more or less excluded from public transport.

If we ask disabled people (and we have been asked in various surveys) how many of us feel that we are excluded from public transport, the answer is around 4 per cent of the population. There are over two million of us who say that we cannot use public transport, or can use it only with extreme difficulty.

Special transport provision

There is some special provision, around the country. Various initiatives make some parts of public transport accessible to impaired people. However, as Table 1 suggested, the extent of this provision is minimal.

I will use London as an example, for two reasons: because London is relatively well developed in this respect compared to most other parts of Britain, and because there has been considerable research on travel patterns in London. The main forms of accessible public transport in London are Dial-a-Ride (accessible door-to-door minibuses) and Taxicard (subsidies for use of taxis). Table 3 shows that for the 90,000 or so people eligible to use these transport schemes, there are simply so few vehicles that they would allow at most almost one trip a week per person – clearly an unacceptable low level of provision.

Analysis of general travel patterns in London suggests that while about 1.5 million trips a year are made by these two schemes, to give disabled people parity with other people that figure should be about 85 million. This gives some indication of how disadvantaged we are.

Table 3   Numbers of members and trips: London Dial-a-Ride and Taxicard

	Number of members	Number of trips per year	Average no of trips per member per week
London Dial-a-Ride (June 94)	53,000	800,000	0.30
London Taxicard 92/93	40,000	700,000	0.35
Total	93,000 (overlap)	1.5m	0.65 (max)

Note: There are in addition other admirable initiatives in London, for example accessible bus services in Hounslow and Ealing and elsewhere, but the amount of provision is minuscule.

Figure 3   Proportions of people who live in different size households, UK

%
50

legend
[illegible] whole population
[illegible] disabled people

25

0

% who live alone   % in h/holds of 3+

Source: 1991 Census

The need for transport
Why we need public transport is a question that only somebody who has never suffered exclusion from public transport could ask. Transport is a basic – if derived – need, a basic good and something which most people would regard as a right in our society. It is a means to the end of satisfying so many other basic needs: employment, socialisation, education and so on.

Transport is fundamental to overcoming isolation. Figure 3 shows that while 50 per cent of disabled people live alone, less than 20 per cent of adults in the whole population do; conversely, while 20 per cent of disabled people live in households of three or more people, 40 per cent of the general population do. Isolation is a phenomenon disabled people share with elderly people in general. It follows from this that disabled people's need for socialisation is far greater than other people's; it should come as no surprise that despite this the means to achieve socialisation are scarcer than for the less needy general population – another reflection of our oppression.

The effects of transport disability

The effects on disabled people
Disabled people's exclusion from public transport restricts opportunities in employment, in leisure, in education, for interaction with other

people, in role identity, in self expression through activity.) These restrictions lead via exclusion from these particular areas to far more significant and pernicious effects. We become alienated, we become ill, we become poor and marginalised. And there is a vicious circle which many of us know: exclusion from transport makes it difficult for us to organise to fight against that very exclusion. It is difficult for disabled people to get together to form groups to fight against the very thing which prevents us grouping. Community transport has had a role here, bringing disabled people together with others in its community development function.

The effects on the economy

The annual costs to the economy of excluding disabled people from public transport have been recently estimated to be as high as £1 billion per year. Table 4 – taken from the recent report *Cross Sector Benefits of Accessible Public Transport*[4] – shows how this total has been derived.

The argument made in that report is that if society excludes disabled people from public transport, society incurs a great deal of expenditure as a result. Examples of this range from the extra costs of bringing chiropody services to our homes because we can't go to chiropody clinics, to the effects of exclusion from public transport on our employment opportunities.

Table 4   Annual costs of bringing services to people denied access to public transport (UK)

£ millions

Activity	Transport disability costs (high estimate) pa
Chiropody	5
Meals	10
GPs	67
Home care	141
Other domiciliary care	38
Social work	61
Residential to day care	163
Employment	650
Patient transport services	26
Total per year	1,161

The government (two of whose ministers signed the foreword to the report) would do well to remember, when estimating the cost of civil rights legislation, that investing in access to public transport can have pay offs in the order of savings on other services of £1 billion every year.

Why is public transport inaccessible?

Historical analyses of this question may be found elsewhere. What is clear is that the current perpetuation of inaccessibility relates to inherent values of free market philosophy – belief in strong self-sufficient individuals, unwillingness to subsidise public services, commitment to deregulation and competitive tendering and in general hostility to anti-discrimination legislation. In transport terms this reveals itself in the supremacy of that wonderful vehicle, the private car, the ultimate symbol of possessive individualism. Transport subsidy is massively skewed away from trains and buses and public transport towards cars and the roads and motorways that support them.

In the area of public transport legislation I am aware of only one public transport authority in Britain – London Transport – that has any legal duty to provide transport for disabled people. A campaign by disabled people forced a Lords amendment to the London Regional Transport Act 1984 upon a very unwilling government.

How is public transport controlled?

It is important if we are going to try and affect public transport that we know where decisions are made. Figure 4 resembles a tree diagram. Its roots are public transport operators who are generally private limited companies operating for profit. In general they get the majority of their working capital and funds from fares and a minority from subsidies.

In the competitive deregulated transport environment outside London the principal role transport authorities are obliged to take is in the provision of socially necessary services, where a requirement for access could be a condition of contracts with providers. For the competitive network there is no requirement to provide accessible services; they are registered by a traffic commissioner whose role is mainly confined to ensuring safe operation through the operator licensing system.

Above these authorities is the Department of Transport which supports public transport, mainly by allowing local authorities to raise money to finance public transport capital projects but also by funding

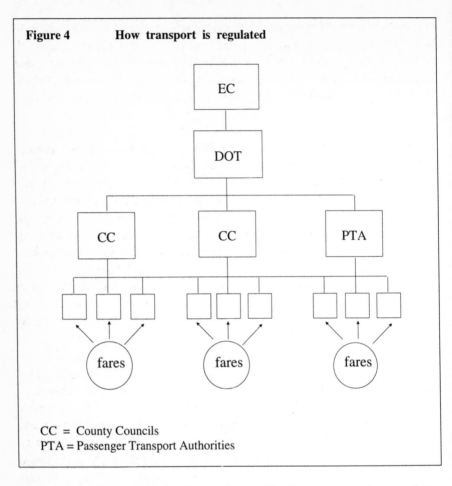

Figure 4 **How transport is regulated**

CC = County Councils
PTA = Passenger Transport Authorities

some – mainly experimental – projects. The Department also regulates the operation of public transport in the UK.

Above the Department of Transport we have Europe: the European Commission and the European Parliament. These bodies promulgate regulations – which are not always in harmony with what the Department of Transport advocates – and also fund special projects.

The Department of Transport has targets for the accessibility of public transport; almost all are statements of good intent. There are no targets of the sort disabled people would like to see such as 'x per cent of all public transport shall be accessible by y date'. These do not exist in the Department's official programmes. There is, though, a commitment to having all London taxis accessible by the year 2000. A helpful target and not to be denigrated; nevertheless I think it is curious that the Department's one firm target for accessible transport relates to a form of transport that many people would not immediately think of as 'public', and has been considered the preserve of rich people rather than the ordinary public. Access in terms of personal finances and the taxi fleets' operating methods are critical; nevertheless, taken together with the London boroughs' subsidy of disabled people's use of taxis there is no doubt that the initiative is a success.

There is also a commitment to subsidise and encourage the introduction of low floor buses in London. London Transport already have 68 vehicles in operation or planned and are inviting bids to run further routes with low-floor buses as each route is subjected to the competitive tendering procedure.[5] To put this in perspective, there is a total of well over 5,000 buses operating in London. In addition, the Department of Transport does have a commitment to not funding any major new transport projects in the country which are inaccessible. However, when we look at the Department's total funding, we find that it currently spends nearly £6 billion a year on funding transport across the UK – approximately £120 per person; in London they spend £12 million on Dial a Ride – approximately £24 for each of the estimated half-million[6] transport-handicapped Londoners.

One hopeful development is that the Department of Transport has taken the cross-sector benefit idea seriously. It obviously helps those people within the Department who are in favour of and committed to accessible public transport; in an inter-departmental working party which is exploring the idea of cross-sector benefits, the Department of Transport is arguing that the Departments of Health, Social Security and Employment should transfer money into funding accessible public transport in order to save money in their traditional budgets. This working party is working towards a policy statement on the implications for government of cross-sector benefits, and this in turn – at the very least – should mean that new major pieces of social policy or social engineering will not ignore transport in the way that for example community care policy has. (However, the London Borough of Ealing's Community Care Plan does give an example of how transport can be integrated into community care planning.)

The costs of making public transport accessible

I do not know of any definitive study which has estimated the cost of making public transport accessible throughout the UK. Nor am I sure that this would be important, because I think any definitive study would be far in advance of our prospects of achieving it at the moment. I do, however, believe that a lot of the spectres that are raised in this respect – such as the wild overestimates in recent costings of the Disabled Persons' Bill – are indeed spectres.

On the one hand these estimates completely miss out the cost-benefit analysis – the cross-sector benefit argument. On the other, they raise the phantom of completely scrapping and replacing the transport stock, rather than phased replacement as stock wears out. In a report in 1993 the Office of Technology Assessment of the Congress of the United States said on the subject of accessible buses:

> ... to implement level-change devices for each new bus will cost ...
> approximately 1 per cent of total operating costs for that vehicle. Assuming
> a 20-year phase-in period, costs to the industry as a whole would rise
> by approximately one twentieth of 1 per cent per year.[7]

It is just as Andrew Walker points out in his chapter on architectural barriers: the cost of making a bus accessible – like the cost of an accessible dwelling – if you get it right in the design, is negligible; and of course the benefits are enormous.

Another kind of cost or resource problem is where you start. It is not a lot of good having one accessible bus on a bus service and then expecting it to be fully used. Until most of the buses are accessible disabled people simply will not go to the bus stop. This is common sense – but common sense and planning somehow do not always seem to go together. Access to public transport is an issue which I do not believe can be solved piecemeal. It needs to be solved by regulation and by government policy.

Transport planning may be rather specialised, but we have done some work developing a methodology for evaluating investment in transport to reflect the needs of people. Current transport planning tends to be based on demand. At its most absurd it would count the number of people in wheelchairs waiting for buses in order to measure the transport needs of wheelchair users. Not surprisingly, the need for wheelchair access is not one of the things that comes out of that approach.

But it is quite possible to develop a proper methodology for transport planning that reflects need as distinct from demand. It takes account of travel need in terms of (i) how much travel people do (ii) how isolated the group is and (iii) how much they need to travel, together with travel costs in terms of (iv) how much it costs to provide transport for people in that particular group (v) the size of that group relative to the total population; from this it derives a methodology for allocating resources (see Figure 5).

Figure 5 **Components of a formula for needs-based allocation of transport funding**

Travel need (a)
- the difference between the average amount travelled by
  (i) the population in general and
  (ii) the group in question;
  defined as the % improvement given by, say, an extra four trips per week.

Travel need (b)
- the extent of social isolation of the target group; defined by reference to a hierarchy of needs from
  (i) affiliative (interaction with significant others), through
  (ii) occupational (active role identity), to
  (iii) self-achievement (self-expression through activity).

Travel cost (c)
- unit cost of accessing transport for an individual in the group in question.

Travel cost (d)
- the size of the group relative to the total population.

Source: Alex Bruce, Camden Needs-Based Transport Planning Group, 1985

What is to be done?

I take it as axiomatic that travel need is not something which ought to be solved by individual effort. I believe that transport provision should be sorted at the level of public transport – nationally and by government. Historically public transport has been designed to exclude disabled people: this is the position our analysis starts from. This exclusion will not change without some force for change, and that force has either got to be economic or regulatory. I cannot expect economic forces for change in the sense that individual disabled people will have such spending power that transport operators will woo our custom. Although, having said that, we have talked to transport operators who have said that the number of people using public transport is declining, and any new market they can find is advantageous; as one commercial director put it:

> If the additional features fitted to our Group's buses can reduce that decline by only one per cent then we have a more stable and better business than our competitors.[8]

However I do not hold out too much hope of this solution: it is too big a problem. It has to be solved by regulation, and I think that regulation has to come either from Europe or from the UK government. But regulation is a framework for the solution, and not the solution itself. Regulation will force operators to provide access: there is then a need for a closeness to users and potential users – choice, sensitivity and variety – that is beyond the ability of the farebox relationship to deliver.

I believe there are both hopeful and unhopeful signs from Europe. The unhopeful sign is that the European Commission is favouring promulgating a standard for public transport construction which is worse than that in any member country. The hopeful sign is that the meeting of ministers of transport of European countries is adopting standards which are extremely positive and extremely helpful to us. I believe that there is an opportunity for pressure in support of that standard. (Also, since this was first written, it has become clear that Transport Commissioner Kinnock is a powerful and progressive ally.)

As for the UK government, we obviously need targets for accessible transport. We need a commitment to accessible transport which the government has only the most vague terms at the moment. The *Summary of a Consultation on Government Measures to Tackle Discrimination Against Disabled People* says:

> Discrimination would be outlawed in a variety of areas, including ... facilities for transport and travel, except where existing physical barriers prevent access.[9]

It is not clear to me what that means in terms of change, although it is widely feared that it means very little at all. I think that what we clearly need to do is to press the government to have realistic targets for access to public transport through anti-discrimination legislation which would bear on transport, and through Department of Transport targets.

There are other kinds of minor but not inconsiderable opportunities. Although they are somewhat piecemeal I will mention two of them. One is the needs of rural communities. I have been very struck by the extent of transport deprivation among people outside towns and cities, and it may be that this will increase the pressure for a better and different sort of transport provision. So long as the solution is not always seen in people getting their own cars (which cannot be a viable way forward for the whole population) this may as the needs of rural communities are better articulated lead to better, more user-friendly forms of transport.

The other hopeful development is the potential – in some cases real – effects of the purchaser/provider split. This is leading to the breakdown of traditional distinctions between providers of different services. For example, traditional ambulance services are being deconstructed and already in London health authorities have transferred money to purchasing non-emergency patient transport from alternative providers with the result that they are actually funding patient transport integrated with other community-type operations. There are now accessible small buses going round the London Borough of Camden picking up able bodied and disabled people alike, and their routes include hospitals. Health providers will fund these services because they can achieve an infinitely better standard of transport for people – and at far lower unit costs – than by funding traditional ambulance services.

Finally, the way forward in this as in every other particular aspect of our oppression has to be through organisations of disabled people, those that specialise in transport matters and those which represent us generally.

References
1   Photographs supplied by London Transport Disabled Passengers Unit
2   Department of Transport, *National Travel Survey 1991/93*, HMSO, 1994
3   J Martin, H Meltzer and D Elliot, *OPCS Surveys of Disability in Great Britain, Report 1: The Prevalence of Disability among Adults*, HMSO, 1988
4   A Fowkes, P Oxley and B Heiser, *Cross-Sector Benefits of Accessible Transport*, Cranfield University, 1994
5   London Transport Disabled Passengers Unit (personal correspondence)
6   GLAD, *All Change: A Consumer Study of Transport Handicap in Greater London*, Greater London Association of Disabled People, 1986
7   US Congress, Office of Technology Assessment, *Access to Over-the-Road Buses for Persons with Disabilities*, OTA-SET-547, Washington DC: US Government Printing Office, 1993
8   Fowkes, et al. (as above), p.11
9   DSS Disability Unit, *Summary of a Consultation on Government Measures to Tackle Discrimination Against Disabled People*, HMSO, 1994

6 Employment and disabled people: equal rights or positive action

Caroline Gooding

This is a particularly exciting time to discuss the topic of disability and unemployment since I believe we are at the end of one era and the dawn of a new one. A new ideological framework for addressing the issue, one based on equal rights, is on the verge of being accepted as the basis for policy in this area. The is indicated by the government's proposal in their recent consultative document.[1] They have finally accepted, albeit in a muddled and half hearted way, that a law banning disability discrimination in employment is needed. This is a fundamental shift.

Let me make myself clear. I do not mean to suggest that these proposals in any way represent a firm basis for principled anti-discriminatory policy making. Not only do they completely fail to address the issue of discrimination outside the workplace, but they also reveal a fundamental misunderstanding of the nature of disability discrimination.

It is obvious that this is not a genuine conversion but a response to the pressure of disabled people's campaigning. I take these proposals as a testimony to the impact of our campaign and an indication that we are getting close to our goal of full comprehensive anti-discrimination legislation.

But rather than focusing on the immediate campaigning situation we need to grapple with some underlying principles. In this chapter I consider whether there may be some pitfalls in the equal rights approach, and whether there is anything of value to be retained from the previous era of policy making.

The consultative document proposes that the price for introducing the government's restricted new employment right is the abolition of the quota scheme. There is a great debate as to whether or not we should accept this price. I think that in part this if fuelled by a nervousness about whether equal rights alone can achieve change. It is therefore a particularly opportune time to attempt to unpick some of the issues involved.

Quota and anti-discrimination legislation

The title of this chapter – 'equal rights or positive action' – on one level refers to the two alternative policy models for addressing the issue of disabled people's employment – quotas and anti-discrimination legislation. To date the two approaches appear to be mutually exclusive. There is only one country which combines a specific law banning disability discrimination with a quota scheme – France. In 1990 the existing law making it a criminal offence to discriminate on the basis of race or religion was amended to include discrimination on the basis of disability.[2] However, this is a low-profile measure tacked on to existing policies which appears to have had little impact.

The mutual incompatibility of the two approaches is not surprising given that they stem from different approaches, and from different geographical areas. Thus while the quota scheme is prevalent in Western European countries, equal rights measures feature in English speaking countries of the new world – New Zealand,[3] Australia,[4] Canada[5] and the United States of America.[6]

The development of the quota schemes can be traced to the impact of the First and Second World Wars. Although many of the schemes have been restructured more recently – Germany in 1975, France in 1987 and Italy in 1992[7] – nevertheless their underlying principles derive from this post war era.

In contrast, the development of rights legislation for disabled people is far more recent. The first such measure was introduced in the American Rehabilitation Act 1973, which contained one clause banning disability discrimination in federally funded services, and the most recent is that of New Zealand in 1993.

The different approaches are reflected in the contrasting rationales of the two policies. The quota is fundamentally a collective compensation to individuals for loss of capacity. The impetus for this derives from the state. In contrast the impetus for the rights approach derives from the movements of disabled people themselves, and it does not seek to compensate the individual but to change society by opening it up to disabled people as a whole.

Medical or social model

The explanatory rationale for quotas is the medical model, while for rights it is the social model. Put simply the medical view of disability explains the disadvantages experienced by disabled people as direct consequences of their own physical and functional limitations, whereas the social model emphasises the role of society excluding and disabling individuals.

A recent article in the *Daily Telegraph* vividly illustrates the thinking behind the medical model.[8]

> The only real remedy for disability is a complete cure. Otherwise the best we can do is push many small advantages the disabled person's way, in the hope that their cumulative effect will make up for the original big disadvantage.

In this view equality for disabled people simply does not make sense; it is not an option. The article continues:

> To call that equality, however, is to misuse the language. In place of legs we offer wheels. No number of wheels will ever equal one single leg so how do we know when to stop? The truth is that the disabled cannot manage without the sympathy, indeed the protection, of the rest of society, and they have been badly misled if they think otherwise.

The quota schemes, whether explicitly or implicitly, start from the assumption that disabled people will be less productive than their able-bodied counterparts. In contrast the equal rights model emphasises the role of discrimination.

I will touch very briefly on what the evidence tells us about the validity or otherwise of these two explanation for the disadvantaged position of disabled people in employment.

Looking at the medical model, there is substantial evidence which contradicts its assumption that disabled people are less productive than able-bodied people. The largest ever study of the work performance of disabled people was conducted by the US Department of Labour back in 1948.[9] Comparing the records of 48,000 disabled and able-bodied people it found no difference in productivity, absenteeism or safety records. There have been numerous more recent surveys producing the same results.[10]

On the other hand, turning to the social model, there have been a number of studies illustrating the prevalence of discrimination and its power to exclude disabled people from the workforce. The Spastics Society undertook two investigation several years apart, both using the classic format of two identically qualified applicants presenting themselves for a job, one able-bodied, the other disabled.[11]

In both studies, two out of every five employers turned down the disabled applicant whilst offering an interview to the non-disabled one.

The evidence for the existence of discrimination is the easier to collect because able-bodied people will quite readily express their prejudices. For instance, a survey of physiotherapists found 23 per cent said that people with controlled epilepsy should not work in physiotherapy departments; and a further 22 per cent expressed the same view about people with depression.[12]

Nevertheless, regardless of the evidence of the prevalence of discriminatory attitudes this version of events does not present the whole story.

There are a number of people for whom the labour market presents genuine problems, over and above the operation of attitudinal prejudices and stereotypes. For example

- 21 per cent of disabled solicitors responded to a survey indicating that they thought that physical access problems would disrupt their careers[13] (hardly surprising in the light of the fact that 44 per cent of criminal courts have no wheelchair access and 94 per cent have no facilities for people with hearing impairments). A further 8 per cent indicated that they required special equipment.

- *Employment and Handicap,*[14] a survey of 1,500 disabled people found that:

  - 28 per cent required flexibility in work tasks

  - 22 per cent needed part-time hours

  - 8 per cent reported access difficulties

Now while the explicit concentration of this study on people who fall within the definition of the 1944 Act – that is to say those who are regarded as 'occupationally handicapped' – will have inflated these figures as a proportion of the broader disabled population, nevertheless it is clear that the structuring of the standard working day and working environment do create problems for a small but significant proportion of disabled workers.

It is this issue which recently provoked Colin Lowe to suggest some pitfalls that might befall those endorsing a simplistic version of the social model of disability.[15]

He argued that: 'The underlying assumption of ... the social model of disability is that disabled people are fundamentally no different from non-disabled people. If they are not careful, this can all too easily turn into a denial of the reality of disability – a denial of disability itself'. In particular, he warned against obscuring important functional differences by arguing that disabled people should be treated exactly the same as non-disabled people 'as this then plays into the hands of those who argue that meeting disabled people's "special" needs gives them unfair preference'.

I want to examine this in more detail because it pinpoints a source of the anxiety which some disabled people have about equal rights as the sole instrument of social change: that is the fear that this approach entails treating everyone in an identical way, ignoring the real differences that exist.

Equality and difference: sex and race

I think it is helpful at this point to look at the experience and critiques of groups which already have experience of the equal rights approach: black people and women. Both the anti-racist and feminist criticisms of equal rights legislation warn against the classic model of equal rights. This model seeks to remedy the long and entrenched history of discrimination against black people and women by banning future acts of discrimination, and in particular by requiring that all individuals should receive identical treatment. This formalistic model of equality dictates that groups which have been excluded by prejudice should be given the same opportunities as those who have already benefited from inclusion in the mainstream.

However, the problem with this model is that it ignores institutionalised discrimination, the legacies of historical exclusion and also continuing discrimination in areas of life outside the workplace.

It is premised on the existence of a neutral-functioning, non-discriminatory society in which only isolated acts of discrimination occur.

A leading Afro American critic of this model argues that it thus 'leads us to think about racism in a way that advances the disease rather than combating it'.[16] He suggests that by 'insisting that a blameworthy perpetrator be found before the existence of racial discrimination can be acknowledged, the [law] creates an imaginary world where discrimination does not exist unless intended. By acting as if this imaginary world was real ... the law ... subtly shapes our perception of society ... If blacks are being fairly treated yet remain at the bottom of the socioeconomic ladder, only their inferiority can explain their subordinate position.'

Just as the failure of such a model reinforces racist prejudices, so if applied to disabled people it will strengthen the view that the cause of the disproportionately low wages and unemployment amongst disabled people is their own inherent lack of capabilities – their impairments.

A model of equality which ignores the operation of institutional or structural discrimination transposes the problems created by these structures into problems blamed on individuals. It is because an individual differs from the white able-bodied norm that they do not fit in and are thus inappropriate for the job. This is seen as the black or female or disabled individual's fault; the structures which create an in-built advantage for white able-bodied men are not questioned. As one feminist critic put it: 'the relevant differences have been, and always will be, those which keep women in their place'.[17]

The formal model of equality is, however, supplemented in our anti-discrimination laws by other aspects which attempts to address precisely this issue, and which might be said to be based on a substantive model of equality, capable of addressing issues of difference.

Just to illustrate the sort of issues of difference which may confront racial minorities, and how they have been addressed in law, a leading American case involved an employer who demanded a high school diploma for unskilled jobs.[18] The acknowledged inferiority of education received by black children in the Deep South meant that far fewer black applicants had such diplomas. Because this level of qualification bore no relevance to the jobs in question the court ruled that this criteria was unfairly discriminatory. Even though there was no intention to discriminate, the result was the same, and could not be justified by business necessity.

I would like to quote a key passage from this case because it illustrates very neatly the parallels that can be drawn with the situation of disabled people. The judgement said 'Congress has now provided that tests or criteria for employment ... may not provide equality merely in the sense of the fabled offer of milk to the stork and the fox. On the contrary Congress has now required that the posture and condition of the job seeker be taken into account. It has – to resort again to the fable – provided that the vessel in which the milk is proffered be one all seekers can use.'

To take another example, one of the key historical legacies of discrimination for women is occupational segregation. The overwhelming majority of women are still concentrated into a handful of occupations – clerical, cleaning, catering and shopwork. This then allows the other, better-paid occupations to be structured to suit men. Dickens describes as the 'key to women's disadvantage in the labour market' the fact that 'the structures of employment, although apparently neutral, are in fact moulded around the life patterns and domestic obligations of men'.[19] Women's double shift does not fit – part-time work is almost invariably female work – 87 per cent of part-timers are women. The hours of many 'male occupations' form a barrier to women's participation.

From these two examples it is clear that the barriers to participation among so-called minority groups in many instances overlap. Part-time work suits women and some disabled people; and conversely easy physical access to facilities benefits not only disabled people but also people with push-chairs and heavy shopping – who are predominantly female. And, in fact, changing certain features in the workplace (for example by introducing flexible hours) can benefit all workers and arguably employers as well.

I have gone into this area in some detail because many commentators argue that the issue of difference sets disabled people off from other so-called minority groups. In the words of one author: 'The most significant difference between the handicapped and other protected status may also affect their performance.' I would argue that this may also be the case with other disadvantaged groups if the existing work and social environment is taken as a given.

Positive action or quota?

It is also helpful to learn from these groups' experience with equal rights laws that, while the narrow approach to achieving equality has significantly failed, other legal approaches have proved capable of addressing the problem. The most powerful of these is positive action programmes.

The broader historical and social disadvantages suffered by certain groups means that merely imposing minimal standards of non-discriminatory conduct is not sufficient to promote anything like equality in practical terms. That is to say that while it may result in equal treatment, it will not achieve genuinely equal opportunities, or equal outcomes, for disadvantaged groups.

The most effective legal mechanism for achieving equal opportunities has been affirmative or positive action.[20] These programmes may be adopted voluntarily, ordered by a court or imposed as a condition of a state contract – so-called contract compliance. They have been much more widely practised in America than Britain, and to considerable effect. Affirmative action was practised for a short period in Britain through the adoption of contract compliance policies by some local authorities.[21] The Canadians have the Employment Equity Act which requires large employers to survey their workplace and prepare positive action plans.

Affirmative action has been associated in popular consciousness with quotas – but it is in fact a broader and more complex attempt to remedy the exclusion of disadvantaged groups, with the goal of achieving a more balanced workforce, more representative of society at large. It may involve setting targets, fixed on the basis of what might be expected to happen in the absence of discrimination, to assist in monitoring the results of the affirmative action programme.

In the words of the Commission for Racial Equality: 'The only way in which the presence of racial discrimination, including covert and unintentional acts, can be routinely revealed is the ethnic monitoring of certain decisions. The whole experience of the Commission points to the central conclusion. No organisation can be sure that racial discrimination is not occurring unless it has such as system in place.'[22]

Positive action entails analysing and addressing the barriers to the participation of certain groups of workers – be these inflexible hours, lack of physical access or qualifications which are in practice irrelevant for the job. A wide variety of different actions may be included within a positive action programme – from targeted recruitment or advertising to remedial training and child care provision. For disabled people it might, in addition, include adapting the physical environment and restructuring jobs.

In the sense that such policies entail focusing on the difference between the disadvantaged groups and the white able-bodied norm and, at times, treating groups differently precisely on the basis on these defining characteristics, such policies diverge sharply from the classic formal equality model.

We have returned, via a circuitous route, to the issue of quotas. However, the crucial distinction is that when targets are set as part of an affirmative action programme this is within the equal rights framework. Its rationale is redressing the effects of past exclusion and discrimination, and it operates by attempting to alter the structural barriers.

In contrast, the rationale for European quotas for disabled workers was collective guilt, operating by compensating the individuals with jobs. These differing rationales translate into important practical differences. While the targets within affirmative action plans are merely a means of measuring the success of programmes in opening up the workplace, fulfilling the quota, is seen as an end in itself. Any old job will do in terms of meeting the quota, whereas affirmative action plans are concerned to address the discriminatory practices which restrict disabled workers to the lower grades.

Affirmative action needs to be established alongside and on the basis of laws to combat discrimination – both inside and outside the workplace. In comparison, the European quotas exist on their own, in place of equal rights laws, and are confined to the workplace.

Potency of rights discourse

The other crucial distinction between quota systems and equal rights is that only the state can enforce the quota; disobedience is seen as a crime against the authority of the state.

In the equal rights approach, the injury is understood as being against the disabled individuals and they themselves are able to take legal action.

While it is important that the state, or some other agency, exists to provide strategic enforcement powers, it is vital that disabled people are themselves able to initiate legal action.

In practical terms, this acts as a counter to any reluctance on the state's part to enforce the law. In term of the ideological message conveyed by the law, the distinction is every bit as important. Disabled people's power to act on their own behalf, rather than being dependent on the state, is recognised and reinforced. In the potent words of one of the commentators: 'For the historically disempowered, the conferring of rights is symbolic of all the denied aspects of humanity: rights imply a respect which places one within the referential range of self and others which elevates one's status from human body to human being.'[23]

Written from a black feminist perspective, these words apply with equal force to disabled people who have for so long had their humanity denied, and been deprived of the capacity for self-determination.

Once again, the process is as important as the end result. Articulating a common right to equal access has proved tremendously important for the individual and collective empowerment of disabled people. Where previously disabled people were taught to experience their subordination in terms of the incapacities of their own bodies, in contrast an understanding that this experience stems from a deprivation of social rights locates the problem in the public sphere.

The common goal and shared activity of asserting a right – the struggle to obtain and implement a legislation – promotes a sense of collective identity among disabled people who, despite the vast differences of their individual disabilities, share a common experience of exclusion and stigmatisation. A rights discourse also promotes the positive self-identification of disabled people. In the past, because of the historical stigma attached to disability, many people denied the label. President Roosevelt, for example, went to great lengths to conceal the impact of polio, but as a wheelchair user he undoubtedly experienced the powerful impact of social exclusion and stigma. As disability comes to be understood in terms of discrimination, rather than as a personal failing, and as the stigma attached to the label becomes weaker, more people will be prepared to accept it.

Thus, President Bush, when endorsing the Americans with Disabilities Act, acknowledged his personal interest in the law, as the father of two disabled sons.

In the end, I would argue that the ideological message conveyed by a law is almost as important as its direct, practical effect. The equal rights perspective has tremendous potential for empowering disabled people, and positively shaping the broader social discourse. As a feminist writer has pointed out, 'the very act of couching a claim in terms of rights rather than needs is a major step towards a recognition of a social wrong'.[24]

A rights discourse transposes problems into ones which have social and legal solutions. As long as the exclusion, segregation and second class status of disabled people is seen as their individual problem, caused by their own physical or mental impairment, the solution will continue to be posed in terms of a medical cure or charitable dependency. To recast the issue in terms of structural discrimination is to present the solution as a change to society not to the individual.

The need for synthesis

Having attacked the assumptions and operation of the quota schemes, and somewhat one-sidedly sung the praises of the equal rights approach, I would like to end by emphasising the importance of supplementing this approach with one of the key ideological under-pinnings of quota schemes: the acceptance of collective responsibility. The formal model of equal rights focuses purely on the individual's right not to experience discrimination. This right is characteristically asserted against another individual or a company, with the state playing a neutral role. The only claim made against the state is a purely negative one: that the state should stop discriminating against the individual.

However, achieving the positive goal of equal access to social institutions (as opposed to the negative goal of ending discrimination) requires the active intervention of the state. I have already mentioned the importance of the state assisting in the implementation of equality laws. It also needs to provide resources to assist private entities to remove barriers. Achieving equality means changing the status quo, and this can mean disruption and expense.

The state should accept its role in smoothing out the transition. An acknowledgement of collective responsibility for change is thus the necessary basis for an effective legal solution.

Specifically, there is the need for a broad range of government assistance to employers to enable them to dismantle barriers and meet the additional needs of disabled employees. This would reduce the costs imposed on individual employers, recognising that the exclusion of disabled workers from the workforce is a social problem, and that redressing the situation is a social priority. This may be done with tax incentives, as in America, or by direct funding, as currently occurs in Britain under the Access to Work schemes. This state-funded programme provides a wide range of support, including payments for interpreters for deaf people and personal assistants for physically disabled people, as well as funding adaptations to buildings.

The funding of sickness leave and disability leave, where needed, is as important an underpinning of equal rights, as the funding of maternity leave is for women's equality. While many disabled people have no additional requirements for time off, others may have; and even those who do not need it are adversely affected by employer's common perception that disabled people will take more time off due to illness.

What I am arguing is that governments need to supplement an equal rights approach by providing positive rights to the additional resources required by disabled people, both inside and outside the workplace. Outside the workplace, some disabled people will have significant additional costs associated with their disability which they will rarely be able to afford from their wages. These additional expenses need to be met by the state in a way which does not jeopardise the participation of disabled people in the labour market. Put simply, people should not be worse off because they work.

Far from such a positive rights approach, the state welfare system currently represents one of the most significant barriers to disabled people entering the workforce.

Furthermore, to claim disability specific benefits – such as incapacity benefit or severe disablement allowance – disabled people have to show that they are incapable of work, and this is an all or nothing test, which does not recognise that many disabilities prevent full-time work but allow part-time work. The benefit system makes it very difficult for disabled people to work part-time without great loss of income.

Conclusion

It is vital that we recognise the strengths of the two traditions – the welfare state or collectivist tradition of Western Europe, from which the quota scheme flows, and the equal rights tradition, which is strongest in the USA.

There is a danger that arguments focused on integrating disabled people into work could be used as a justification for withdrawing welfare benefits, and dismantling the welfare state, on the basis that 'they are all equally able to work now'.

We need to ensure that instead of the equal rights argument being used to undermine collective provision, it is used to improve it, so that an ethos of entitlement and a goal of supporting disabled people in work are used to restructure the welfare state system. The greatest asset in this endeavour is the collective mobilisation of disabled people, which I believe is also the greatest strength of the equal rights approach.

Notes

1   *Disability on the Agenda: A Consultation on Government Measure to Tackle Discrimination against Disabled People,* DSS, 1994
2   For an overview on international legislative frameworks see N Lunt and P Thornton, *Employment Policies for Disabled People: A Review of Legislation and Services in Fifteen Countries,* Social Policy Research Unit, University of York, 1993; and for a discussion of the ethos of the quota schemes see M Floyd, 'Overcoming Barriers to Employment', in G Dalley (ed) *Disabilitiy and Social Policy* PSI, 1990
3   Human Rights Act 1993
4   Disability Discrimination Act 1992
5   Canadian Human Rights Act 1977
6   Americans with Disabilities Act 1990
7   *Up to Standard? Employment Quotas for Disabled People in Other Countries,* TUC, 1994

8 'The Disabled Have Rights But So Do the Rest of Us', *Daily Telegraph*, 24 May 1994

9 *The Performance of Physically Impaired Workers in Manufacturing Industry*, US Department of Labor, 1948

10 *Disability and Discrimination*, RADAR, 1994

11 E Fry, *An Equal Chance or No Chance: A Study on Discrimination in Employment*, Spastics Society, 1986; P Graham, A Jordan and B Lamb, *An Equal Chance or no Chance*, Spastics Society, 1990

12 Reported in *Therapy Weekly*, Vol.19, No.17, October 1992

13 P Jenkins, 'The Training and Work Experience of Solicitors with Disabilities', *Educare*, No.44, October 1992

14 P Prescott Clarke, *Employment and Handicap*, Social Community Planning Research, 1990

15 C Lowe, 'The Social Model of Disability', *Rehab Network*, No.32, Winter, 1993

16 C Lawrence, 'The Id, Ego and Equal Protection: Reckoning with Unconscious Racism', *Stanford Law Review*, Vol.39, January 1987

17 A Scales, 'The Emergence of Feminist Jurisprudence', *Yale Law Journal*, Vol.95, June 1986

18 Griggs v Duke Power Co 1971

19 L Dickens, *Whose Flexibility? Discrimination and Equality Issues in Atypical Work*, Institute of Employment Rights, 1992; R Burggdorf and C Bell, *Accommodating the Spectrum of Abilities*, US Commission for Civil Rights, 1983

20 E Meehan, *Women's Rights at Work: Campaigns and Policy in Britain and the United States*, Macmillan, 1985; C Gooding, *Disabling Laws, Enabling Acts: Disability Rights in Britain and America*, 1994

21 *Contract Compliance – The UK Experience*, Institute of Personnel Management, Income Data Services, 1987

22 *Second Review of the Race Relations Act*, Commission for Racial Equality, 1992

23 P Williams, 'Alchemical Notes: Reconstructing Ideals from Deconstructed Rights', *Harvard Civil Rights – Civil Liberties Law Review*, Vol.22, Spring 1987

24 E Schneider, 'The Dialectic of Rights and Politics: Perspectives from the Women's Movement', *New York University Law Review*, Vol.61, October 1986

This chapter is based on the book *Disabling Laws, Enabling Acts: Disability Rights in Britain and America*, by Caroline Gooding, Pluto Press, 1994.

7 Social security, poverty and disabled people

Richard Berthoud

Our research suggests that half of all the disabled people in the country are poor.[1] I could go into more detail and explain the methods of measurement by which I reach that conclusion, but I do not want to do that. What I conclude from that statistic is that a very large number of disabled people have very little money to live on. Most of them live on benefits. The question is, how could the social security system enable them to have more money to live on, so that there would be no question of whether they were poor or not.

The disability lobby has for many years been campaigning in various ways for some form of comprehensive disability income scheme. This is a useful political tactic in which a whole package of reforms is proposed. I do not want to propose another disability income scheme of my own; what I want to do is to talk about the different elements of social security that are of greatest importance to disabled people. Basically there are three elements which need to be looked at. One is earnings replacement; the second is benefits which deal with the additional cost of living for disabled people; and the third is benefits which encourage work rather than simply replace earnings for those who have no employment.

In Chapter 2 Mike Oliver says that our welfare system encourages dependence, and indeed it does. That will be the last section of this chapter – about how social security might do something to improve work incentives. But there is a basic problem – whatever aspect of social security we are talking about – in the conflict between welfare and incentives. If you think that people who are not in work should be given plenty of money to live on, because it is not their fault they have not got a job, then you are for their *welfare*. But the more money you give to people who are not in work because they need it, the greater the difficulty of trying to square the circle and also create incentives and be fair to people in work. So the problem of dependence is not something which will go away.

Another major issue for social security for disabled people is to what extent should disabled people have access to a special system of benefits for them and for them only; or should they take their luck with everybody else and just claim ordinary benefits? You can see immediately that there is a conflict here. If disabled people did have a special system they would get more money, so they might want a special system. But, on the other hand – and again I refer to Mike Oliver's chapter – that may be a segregating system. People have to plead specially that they need extra money because they are disabled. Then they have to go through tests; they have to emphasise what they cannot do rather than the contribution they can offer. The risk is that they may be encouraged to adopt a 'disabled' identity.

Earnings replacement benefits

There is no doubt at all that people who have impairments have great difficulty in getting jobs; and the greater their impairment the greater the difficulty. Chart 1 shows this for men (the pattern is very similar for women, but is more complicated, so I shall simply use men to illustrate the findings). About 80 per cent of non-disabled men of working age are in employment. Measuring people's impairments is not straightforward, but the OPCS scale shows that, the greater their impairments, the less likely they are to have a job. So only 10 per cent of the most severely impaired men are in work.

I have tried to word that quite carefully. There are two different explanations. As Caroline Gooding explains in Chapter 6, the medical model would say 'they cannot work'; the social model would say 'they are being excluded from work'. But one way and another they are not working and they have not got an income from work. The social security system has to address the question of how much money they should receive. So it is important that there should be an earnings replacement element in any disablement income system. The next question is how much this basic benefit should be. In the next section I discuss the additional costs of disability, so I am simply concerned now with the part that compensates for the fact that people have no job.

The question is whether disabled people should receive the same as unemployed people – which is the lowest rate of benefit available in the system – or whether (as most of them do at the moment) they should receive rather more. Inevitably when discussing social security

Chart 1   Proportion of men in employment, by severity of impairment

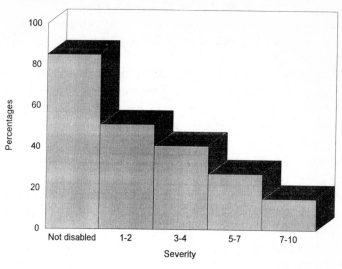

Source: Secondary analysis of OPCS disability survey; Berthoud, Lakey and McKay, 1993

benefits, we are talking about quite small amounts of money. The difference is between about £50 per week unemployment benefit and £70 a week invalidity benefit – well short of average earnings levels. But should disabled people claim the ordinary benefit for unemployed people because they ought to participate in the same scheme as everyone else? Or should they get rather more, because of the particular problems that they have experienced in obtaining work? One could put the argument the other way: why is it that unemployed people get less than disabled people? Disabled people get about the same benefit as pensioners, and pensioners are by far the largest group of social security claimants in the country. So you could argue that basic benefit is the pension, which many disabled people can claim; and that unemployed people are discriminated against in order to create incentives to make them work. But you will recognise that there are a lot of arguments here about whether people are unemployed by their own fault or whether they are unable to get jobs.

Then the question is bound to arise for disabled people who can expect no work at all over very long periods: should there be some addition over and above basic benefit levels to make their incomes nearer those of other families. Again, equity between different social security claims is very important. I often talk to audiences of people who are particularly interested in disability; but then I also talk to people who are particularly interested in families with children, or unemployed people and so on. So this question of equity across groups is quite a difficult one. You may notice I am not giving the answer. I am just saying that there is a problem.

One way of making sure that disabled people could get more than basic benefits would be to have an insurance system which allowed for additional money which people had paid for through extra contributions. The state earnings related pension scheme offered just such a bonus to disabled people. It was promising to be quite successful – so the government has abolished it. It was starting to cost a great deal of money. Would we want to bring it back? It was good for the people who had been employed during most of their lives; but people who had not been employed, particularly those who had been impaired from birth and never got into the labour market, could not get into the insurance system either. So, there is another question of equity between different groups of people.

If benefits for disabled people are going to be different from those for unemployed people then there must be some form of assessment to decide who gets the extra rate of benefit for disabled people and who does not. We cannot avoid this. As you know, the method by which the social security system assesses whether people are 'incapable of work' has just been changed. While many members of disability groups are beginning to feel that progress is being made towards a greater awareness of the social construction of disability, the government has actually gone in the opposite direction. The Department of Social Security is in future going to confine its assessment to 'medical' factors: physical, sensory and mental impairments. No consideration will be given to any of the economic, social and environmental factors which help to decide whether *this* disabled person is in fact able to get a job in the real world. So on this aspect of policy we are going backwards.[2]

Extra costs benefits

There is a second set of benefits which applies only to disabled people. Again if you are to have a special system for disabled people, that is a crucial part of it. A lot of the argument over the past few years was an empirical one, a research one, as to how much extra it actually costs to live in a disabling world, and what the extra costs consist of. I want to divide that question into routine living expenses, the sort of things that everyone has to spend money on like food and fuel and so on but which disabled people might have to spend more on; and things which only disabled people have to pay for, like wheelchairs or personal assistance.

The story about how the extra costs of disability have been measured is now a familiar one.[3] The Office of Population Censuses and Surveys asked some direct questions, and came up with the answer that in today's money the extra cost for the most severely impaired people was about £20 a week.[4] A lot of people did not believe it could be as low as that, so the Disablement Income Group did their own survey and came up with the answer that in today's money it was about £100 a week.[5] Another group of people could not believe that people whose total income was only about £100 a week were spending it all on the special costs of disability, and none on ordinary living costs. Our own research [6] was based on a comparison of living standards. We estimated that the extra costs associated with severe impairments were about £50 a week. Not only can I justify the empirical methods by which we reached that answer, but also it is credible in a way that the other two perhaps were not.

Now, how do current benefits match up to that? Of course, there are many details of the current system which one would take issue with. There was a huge administrative cock-up when the disability living allowance was brought in. That was a serious issue at the time, but not a long-term one. Another serious issue is that elderly people are still deprived of the mobility component of DLA.

A more general point is illustrated by Chart 2. According to our estimates the extra cost of living for the people who are most severely impaired is about £50 a week. If we look at how much attendance allowance and mobility allowance were used to provide to severely impaired people, it came to about £50 a week on average, so that was not bad. But we also found that for people in the middle range of severity, round about grades 5 and 6 on the OPCS scale, the extra costs were of the order of £40 a week. But they were getting less than £10 a week out of the old attendance allowance and mobility allowance, because it was not reaching them so effectively. The Department of Social Security recognised this problem and decided to deliver more money to the middle of the severity scale. But the new DLA manages to deliver only about £1 a week extra. So there was still a big gap in the middle of the disability scale between people's extra costs and the amount of extra income they were getting.

One of the broad issues, about social security as well as about social services, is whether policy should concentrate on the large

Chart 2   Extra costs and additional income of disabled people, by severity

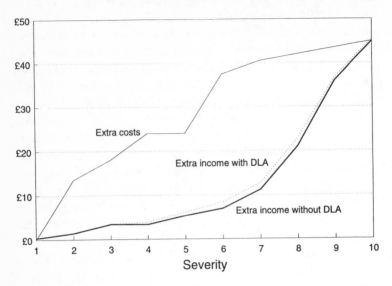

Source: *Secondary analysis of OPCS disability survey;* Berthoud, Lakey and McKay, 1993

numbers of disabled people who are fairly severely impaired, or whether it should concentrate on the very small numbers of people who are very severely impaired. Again that is not something I have an answer to; it is a question that needs to be addressed.

But there are two important points about the disability living allowance. One is that it is not means-tested. What that means is that people can keep the extra income when they move into work and therefore it encourages them to work rather than hindering them. The other important point is that, although there has to be an assessment procedure which says whether you get the benefit and how much benefit you get, you do not have to provide details of your extra needs. Under the old supplementary benefit system, disabled people had to get a doctor's certificate to say they needed three baths a week; they had to get a doctor's certificate to say they needed milk in their diet and so on. That system did not work. Not only did it not work, I think it was demeaning. That is my personal opinion; I suspect it is shared by a lot of other people. It is much better to have rules which entitle claimants to £10 a week, or £50 a week, which they can spend on what they want. That is a better way of dealing with it.

There is, on the other hand, another element of extra costs where I do not think that sort of automatic approach will work – payments for the costs of personal assistance. Individuals' needs are so highly variable and the amounts of money involved are so large, that they really need to be assessed one at a time. Jane Lakey's very interesting book[7] showed how valuable the Independent Living Fund was, not only to the disabled people who received the money but also to their families. Both sides benefited from the fact that the money was paid into their own hands and they had control over how it was spent and who they had to do the work. But I think it does have to be assessed personally. The Independent Living Fund has effectively been abolished. There is a very small replacement fund but very few new people are going to be able to obtain money from it. There are moves afoot to allow social services departments to make payments direct to disabled people for them to spend as they prefer, rather than provide them with home helps and other services direct.

Those are both good ideas, but they should not be confused. A national benefit paid for by central government with a set of broad rules about who should qualify and who should not qualify is one thing; asking social workers within their locally controlled budgets to decide how much assistance people need and then deciding whether to pay cash or services is different. I am not saying that one is better than the other, but they are quite different from each other. Arguments in favour of one do not necessarily apply to the other.

There was quite a serious problem with the Independent Living Fund, and it is not unlikely to affect any future scheme. It is what I call the triple needs test. First, obviously, you need the assistance. That test is unavoidable. Second, the amount of assistance you are deemed to need is very strongly determined by your family circumstances; people who live alone get much more support than people who live with their family, who can contribute some help. Well that sounds right one way round – people who have no family to help them should get more support. But it does not necessarily sound right the other way round – why should people who have family help already in the house get less support? Then the third test is that you have to establish that you have no money of your own. That was certainly in the rules of the Independent Living Fund and I suspect it will be in the rules of most local authority social services direct payment schemes. Disabled people have to establish that they can not afford to pay for the services themselves. Some people think that follows as sure as spring follows winter. But not everyone thinks that; the important point is that disabled people who want personal assistance to enable them to go out to work will lose their personal assistance as soon as they find a job – now they can afford it.

Encouraging employment

That leads neatly to the final set of issues. How can social security benefits be used to support disabled people in work, rather than discourage them from taking employment.

The government is deeply anxious about the huge increase in the numbers of people claiming invalidity benefit; that is why they have changed their policy. Not everyone agrees with the government on everything, but I hope you agree with them on this point, that the huge increase in the numbers of people on invalidity benefit is very worrying indeed. It means an increase of one million disabled people who are not in employment. I do not believe that there are one million more people with impairments. What has happened is that among a fairly constant number of impaired people, fewer and fewer of them are in work. That is worrying for them, just as much as it is worrying for the Treasury. Such research as has been done suggests that the reason for the huge increase in IVB claimants is that it is getting more and more difficult to find a job if you have an impairment. We do not really understand exactly how that has happened. We do know that many of the one and a half million people on invalidity benefit want jobs and feel that they could do a job if one was available. I mentioned poverty right at the beginning – poverty is greatest among those disabled people who are looking for work. So if you could get those people into work, that would have a huge and beneficial effect in reducing the number of people in poverty.

There is a whole range of things that need to be done. My job is to talk about social security, but I do not think any solution will work unless *all* the proposed policies are put in place. A quota scheme is needed; not the current unenforced quota scheme, but some law which effectively obliges employers to do their duty. Anti-discrimination legislation is also needed though, like practically everyone else, I do not think that it will solve the problem on its own. The government's current main policies under the heading of 'rehabilitation' should also be retained – particular assistance offered to individual people, to help them back into the labour market. But the social security system should also be encouraging people into work rather than encouraging them to adopt a disabled identity and live without work. That is to everybody's benefit: the state's and the people concerned, if could be helped to earn their own living.

The ideal system, and one that would not be as expensive as the Treasury instinctively thinks, would be for some kind of partial incapacity benefit. That is for those people who are acknowledged to have particular difficulties of getting into the labour market to receive benefit, whether they have a job or not. It would be a combination of earnings replacement and work incentive, and could be extremely valuable. But I do not have very high hopes of that occurring.

A second-best in-work benefit was introduced quite recently – the disability working allowance. We have recently published a short report explaining why it is that not many people are claiming the disability working allowance.[8] There are one and a half million disabled people not in work. The benefit was designed to help 50,000 of them to get work. It is currently being paid to only 4,000 people. Only about 200 of those had been encouraged to take their job by the availability of DWA. It is only three years since it started, so maybe it will get better. It was introduced during a slump, and perhaps when the longed-for rise in employment comes, a large number of disabled people will be encouraged to take work. But clearly DWA is not going to solve the problem if it operates on such a very small scale.

Perhaps I could end this analysis of benefits and incentives by pointing out an irony. You can claim the disability working allowance if you were receiving one of the benefits based on incapacity for work – invalidity benefit, severe disability allowance or the disability premium on income support. That is how you prove that you are disabled enough to get the benefit. But, under the new rules introduced in April 1995, you will get the new incapacity and other benefits only if it is the official doctor's opinion that you are totally incapable of undertaking any work. So the benefit designed to encourage people to work will in future be available only to those who are not in a position to take advantage of that incentive!

Conclusion

Unlike some of the other broader ranging contributions to this conference, I have dealt with some of the details of the benefit system – what is sometimes disparagingly called the 'plumbing'. Many commentators want to overlook the plumbing and concentrate on the principles. One of the difficulties of social security is that the plumbing *is* the system; it is difficult to talk about the principles without going into detail. I am concerned by the lack of interest in disability benefits in particular. Social security is a fairly specialist subject that people are not particularly interested in unless they are claiming it. Most academics in departments of social policy I know could deliver a lecture on child benefit, but I should think there are no more than five people who could have done what I have aimed to do and talk about the impact of the disability income system.

I think the same is possibly true of many people in the disability movement. I hear people saying the welfare system is inadequate. But they have no concrete and worked-out proposals suggesting how it could be improved. It is my job as a specialist in social security to work out some of these details, but I would like to see much more interaction between researchers, politicians and members of the movement.

Notes and references

1   R Berthoud, J Lakey and S McKay, *The Economic Problems of Disabled People*, Policy Studies Institute, 1993

2   For a full discussion of the relative roles of medical and external factors in the assessment of 'incapacity', see R Berthoud, 'The Medical Assessment of Incapacity: a case study of research and policy', *Journal of Social Security Law*, May 1995

3   See Berthoud, Lakey and McKay, 1993, Chapter 5

4   J Martin and A White, *The Financial Circumstances of Disabled Adults Living in Private Households,* HMSO 1988

5   P Thompson, M Lavery and J Curtice, *Short-changed by Disability*, Disablement Income Group, 1990

6   Berthoud, Lakey and McKay, 1993

7   J Lakey, *Caring about Independence*, Policy Studies Institute, 1994. See also G Zarb and P Nadash, *Cashing in on Independence*, British Council of Organisations of Disabled People, 1994

8   K Rowlingson, and R Berthoud, *Evaluating the Disability Working Allowance*, Policy Studies Institute, 1994

Part Three

Perspectives on the case for anti-discrimination legislation

8 International perspectives and solutions

Rachel Hurst

This chapter is about how disability is being viewed at the international level, the difference in attitudes between the different countries and the different regions of the world. That experience can help us in looking at how we can do things in this country.

First of all I want to read two quotations to show us where we have been and some people's views of how we are going on in the future. This is from a book *Disability Discrimination Law in the United States, Australia and Canada*[1] which recounts all the three laws and how they affect people. There is a beautiful comment by a legal American activist called Timothy Cook who talks about early attitudes to disabled people. He says:

> The public policy of segregating and sterilising children and adults with disabilities was first implemented throughout the nation in the decade surrounding the turn of the century ... the xenophobic hysteria of the era was fuelled by the new 'science' of the eugenics movement and possessed by severe strictures of Social Darwinism dictating the survival of the fittest. The unprecedented flow of new immigration and the uncertainties of an industrial age added to the hysteria. The xenophobic movements took on all the force of state power and focused that force pervasively against African Americans and against people with disabilities. Thus was visited upon both groups the most severe disqualifications imaginable among citizens.

He goes on to chronicle the legislative results of the segregationist ethic:

> Individuals with disabilities were deemed unfit for citizenship under Mississippi law; children with disabilities were deemed unfit for companionship with other children under Washington law; individuals with severe impairments were considered to be anti-social beings as well as a defect which wounds our citizenry a thousand times more than any plague. They were denied the right to serve on juries, to hold public office, to

marry, to work in certain occupations, to attend public school or even to be seen in the street.

What a testimony. It is supposed to have been around the turn of the century and supposedly things are different now. I am not quite sure that they are in Europe. But at the end of the book they say that the analysis of the three legislations amply demonstrates the existence of a real political and legal commitment in advanced western liberal democracies to effective equality for individuals with disabilities.

Well, I think this could be true in some cases. But let us look between those two extremes of xenophobia and the goal of anti-discrimination legislation at what is actually happening.

I would like to divide the world, not into regions, but into sort of political social areas. I see the world – and this is of real relevance to how they treat disabled people – as divided into four main groups. First, the countries which were the old colonial powers: England, France, Germany, Portugal, Spain. Second, the colonies themselves, those which had white settlers: Australia, New Zealand, Canada and America. (The developing world was also colonised but those populations are on the whole ethnic and are struggling against white and northern supremacy.) Third, the socialist countries of the Nordic region – although it is a very small area, I think it is important to look at how they approach the issue of disability. Fourth, we have to look at how the new Central and Eastern European countries are coping with coming out into the world.

My feeling about the old colonial powers is that they treat disabled people in the same way as they used to treat the people within their empires – in a segregating, patronising and professional way. And the legislation, as is shown in earlier chapters, continues that segregation. The colonies with the white settlers had people who were themselves probably fairly radical, even those who went there against their will. Those who went there on purpose were trying to get away from the patronising attitude, trying to get away from the oppression and the poverty that they were experiencing in their own countries – mostly in Europe. So there is a determination for individual freedom which does not really exist in the old colonial powers.

Then we have the small countries of the Nordic regions who, because they are in fact quite small but have a great deal of resources and good (comparatively speaking) stable economies, can afford, or have been able to afford, to give a very high level of services. In many of them disabled people are not confronted on an everyday basis with the same sorts of really heavy discrimination and oppression that we face in countries like the UK. They still face barriers that the public systems are still not accessible to them. But the resources and the provisions that are given to enable individuals to lead relatively mainstream lives – they can go to mainstream schools, they can get jobs comparatively easily – has not created a climate in which disabled people in those countries have got angry. Plus the fact that in these countries, because again they are quite small, the populations are small and the resources are relatively large, governments have been inclined to talk to consumers. It has not been an uncomfortable alliance and in fact governments have supported consumers, and that is another very important issue to remember.

In the developing world, the situation for disabled people is horrendous when you think through the UN's own statistics 98 per cent of disabled people in the developing world receive nothing at all – no services, no money, nothing. So there you have a population – and the disabled population in the developing countries is far greater than any other disability population – who are the poorest of the poor; they are the most segregated; their prime motivation is to eat and to stay alive. Quite a different initiative than for us.

And now we have the Central and Eastern European countries which are emerging from a sort of grand welfare system in that they have never had an opportunity – or most of them have not had an opportunity this century – to think for themselves, to take control of their own lives, whether they are disabled people or non-disabled people; where they have not had any sort of understanding of individual responsibility. But disabled people, unless they were members of the armed forces, have again received very little and, strangely enough, in most of the Central and Eastern European countries, the only provision has been through disabled people's own initiatives, but even so it has been closely monitored and closely dictated by the political authorities.

So we have this tremendous divergence of experience. We all know what has happened and there is more in Chapter 9 about what has happened in the United States, so I shall not go into that in depth. But there has been, because of this coming together of most of these member states in the United Nations, some considerable activity at the international level around disabled people.

Most of the time up until the late 1970s, this activity was still locked into rehabilitation. Anything that the UN did and said was around provision and the World Health Organisation and health and rehabilitation, and in fact that was going to be the focus of the

International Year of Disabled People. But then a major event happened and this was that disabled people at the international level took the situation into their own hands. Gaining experience from the movement in North America, understanding the oppression and the segregation and the isolation and the hell that they were all living in in their own countries, disabled people articulated that disability was not an issue of charity or rehabilitation; it was an issue of human rights. In this country, we had managed to articulate that extremely well through the Union of the Physically Impaired Against Segregation and through individual thinkers and speakers – disabled people all of them, of course – and this international movement of disabled people had a dramatic effect on the United Nations.

The objective for the International Year of Disabled People was the full and equal participation of disabled people in society – a major step forward. Then, in 1983, the United Nations produced the World Programme of Action which set forth in a small booklet recommendations for member states on how they could fulfil this objective of full and equal participation of disabled people. Every member state of the United Nations signed up to that and not one of them did anything about it. And disabled people started their real activity at the United Nations, which as a result started the Decade of Disabled People. Nobody ever really ever heard about it. The Decade was from 1983 until 1992. But in 1987 we had a mid-term evaluation and that showed absolutely clearly that nobody had done anything about the World Programme of Action. The only activities, the only ways forward, had been through disabled people and their own organisations: the spread of the independent living movement within Europe; the start of real community-based rehabilitation; projects at the grass roots by disabled people. That is community-based rehabilitation as far as I am concerned – it is the same thing as independent living in the southern hemisphere. It is disabled people taking control of their lives, working with the local community to ensure their independence and integration.

Something more had to be done, and two countries – Sweden and Italy – tried to push forward a convention at the UN level. A convention would have meant that each country that signed up to that convention could have been taken to the Court of Human Rights if it fell down on non-implementation. Some of you may know that there is a convention on the rights of women, and we wanted a similar one – a convention on the rights of disabled people. If we had had that, we would not be having the rights struggle that we are having now and I think ADA would have gone through even more quickly. But, we did not get that convention and guess who was one of the major opponents? Of course, it was the UK. We struggled for two years for that convention and it was quite clear that we were not going to get it.

So the disability movement at the international level thought again. And again, through the support of countries like Sweden, Canada and Australia, we set up the idea of the UN Standard Rules on the Equalisation of Opportunities for Disabled People. Those Standard Rules were passed in 1993 by the General Assembly of the United Nations and all countries of the United Nations have signed up to them, including the UK. The Standard Rules are not enforceable, but they are a monitoring and evaluation resource on how equalisation of opportunities can be implemented for disabled people in each member state. It covers all the issues we are concerned with. It covers the image of disabled people, in fact that is the first area, which includes attitudes towards disabled people; it covers access to public services and utilities; it covers education; it covers employment; it covers influence in political life; it covers cultural life; it covers training; it covers every area that you can think of. Those Standard Rules also said that there must be a mechanism through which member states can be monitored to see how they are behaving. But of course the UN never has any money, it certainly never has any money for disability. It was only just in September 1994 that enough resources came forward from one or two member states to put into post an ombudsperson who will internationally monitor member states' implementation of the Standard Rules. I am glad to say that ombudsperson, or special rapporteur as he is called, is a blind man from Sweden called Bengt Lindqvist who has been an active and crucial member of the disability movement, both in his own country and internationally. So we have got somebody in the job who is on our side. It does not often happen – especially at the international level. He still will not have any powers to alter countries' behaviour if they do nothing, but international pressure does change people's behaviour quite dramatically.

We also have another mechanism, which is through the Human Rights Commission. Disability is not included in the universal declaration of human rights per se – although it could be argued that we are included because it does say in the preliminary clause that it is 'men, women, etc ... and any other discriminated against group'. In 1975 the UN did produce a Charter on the Human Rights of

Disabled People, but that is not enforceable. In 1990, again with pressure from the disability community, the UN produced a special report on human rights and disability, and this was a major stepping stone. This report outlined in very clear detail the horrendous discrimination that was practised in every single member state. It also outlined to a great extent the violations, the gross violations, that were being carried out – particularly violations against disabled children and disabled women – and the fact that within war and other violent situations disabled people were being totally ignored, as well as being made. And this report did make a major change. Some of you may be aware that every four or five years the UN Human Rights Committee looks at each country's record on human rights. Now they have to look at each country's record on human rights with regard to disabled people also. This is also why BCODP and Liberty have just produced a report, an alternative report on disabled people and human rights in this country, because UK are having to put their report through to the UN Human Rights Committee this year.

Finally, Europe, and I mean the European Union. We are a very odd region because we have now, within the region, an influence and a political structure which no other region in the world has to the same extent. But that has meant nothing for disabled people. In Europe we are not mentioned in the Convention on Human Rights, we can fight on lack of services only through the Court of Human Justice, and the Maastricht Treaty is irrelevant to us – our human rights have not been recognised. But, again, in the last year a dramatic change has taken place and this has been through the influence of disabled people. It has been a major battle, but we are winning. We held a Parliament of Disabled People in December 1993 and in the mainstream parliament, and this changed the attitude of both the European Parliament and the European Commission. For the first time they understood that disability was a human rights issue and not a rehabilitation issue. The elected parliament has now passed a resolution to that effect and in its white paper on social policy it says that there has to be an initiative towards including equalisation of opportunities and anti-discrimination legislation within the new treaties governing the European Union. Now, that is not going to take place until 1996 but we actually have them on our side. That is going to, and has to have, influence on our member states.

Within this country I would like to say that I think the disability movement has played a major role in the whole battle, this whole struggle at the international level, partly because we have been so marginalised here. As a result we have turned ourselves into thinkers and articulators, and that articulation and that thinking about our oppression have been very useful tools. The book that BCODP published in 1991 on disabled people and discrimination in the UK[2] has been the basis for people's thought throughout Europe and in fact there is now going to be a research study throughout Europe based on the findings in that book. It is very important.

All I can say to conclude is that disabled rights is at last creeping up the international agenda on human rights. It is slowly creeping up but it will get to the top only when disabled people get stronger, get louder and get stroppier. We have no time to be polite, to keep saying thank you for small crumbs of support. We have got to demand proper action.

References

1   G Quinn, M McDonagh and C Kimber, *Disability Discrimination Law*, Dublin, Oak Tree Press, 1993
2   C Barnes, *Disabled People in Britain and Discrimination: A Case for Anti-Discrimination Legislation*, Hurst and Co/BCODP, 1991

9   Lessons from the Americans with Disabilities Act

Marca Bristo

This chapter discusses the lessons for Britain from the Americans with Disabilities Act, but to start with I would like to just share a little bit about something that happened to me and how that affected my life and got me involved in the issue of human rights for people with disabilities. It is really rather simple and for those of you with disabilities I am sure you could change the details of my story but it would probably be the same end result.

It is about a grocery store trip in 1978 after I broke my neck and went back home. All the people who had come to see me in the hospital daily were no longer coming, I was lonesome, I wanted my friends and decided I would cook them dinner. I got myself up and into my chair and ventured out to the grocery story which, where I live, was only about two blocks away. I got within seeing distance of the grocery store and looked down and saw a kerb. Determined to cook this dinner I turned around and pushed all the way around the block the other way. Exhausted, I got within seeing distance of the grocery store and saw another kerb. I went home and cried.

That day that kerb was my problem, it was about what I could not do and I was depressed that this was what my life had in store for me. I spent a fair amount of time feeling that way; that those kerbs were my problem, caused by my body that longer worked the way other people's bodies worked. Later I went to California on a business trip and in Berkeley, I did not see those kerbs. On the airplane returning to Chicago I realised that if they could get rid of kerbs in Berkeley, they could get rid of them in Chicago. I looked at those kerbs differently that day. Instead of seeing them as deficiencies in my life, in my body, I saw them as barriers in the built environment around me.

Now fast forward to 1989 and 1990. Now I have two young children. I am at a museum in Chicago, a museum that has just built a brand new major department; my child, my two year old, climbs down off my lap, runs off across the room, a crowd comes between me and the child and I hear my child crying – 'mommy, mommy, mommy'. I rush to get my child as any mother would do to be greeted by five stairs between me and my child. Five new stairs; five stairs that were built subsequent to the laws that said you should not build stairs in new contexts. I could not get to my son. Ultimately a stranger brought him back to me, put him on my lap and we went home.

That was the day in my life, although I dedicated my life to removing barriers, that I got mad as hell and said, 'I'm not going to take it any more'. Those barriers were no longer barriers to me: in fact they are not barriers, they are acts of discrimination; they are wrong and they do not need to be there. The difference is that in 1978 and 1979 there was not a damned thing I could do about those kerbs; in 1990 there was. When I filed my complaint under a city ordinance, the man at the museum screamed at me over the telephone, the most undignified way I have ever been treated, as he said, 'Mrs Bristo, I hardly know what to say to you about your inability to care for your own children'. Fundamentally, those stairs are about the same prejudice that believes I should not have those children because I am not capable of caring for them. I said, 'Sir, my son is two and a half years old, how do you imagine he's gotten to that point, I've been mothering him every day of his life.'

I sound angry. I am angry. Anybody who falls into disability like I did and suddenly experiences this stuff, after the shock they feel the anger. And it is only after years of putting up with it that we start – in order to cope – putting on the blinders that enable us to function and dissipate our anger. I urge you to reclaim your anger. It is important, it is the tool that helped us in America pass this law. And, fundamentally, the most important thing in passing the law was disabled people's ability to get in touch with that outrage; to touch the scar tissue of their lives and expose it to other people; to be vulnerable for the moment; to tell other people what it feels like and that it is wrong. When we speak with members of Congress they say, you know – the techno-garble on widths of doors and how many elevators and the need for this and the cost for that – became irrelevant when the sea of voices were so profound, telling them those individual stories.

So, when I speak about the lessons of the ADA in America, the lessons are right here in this room, in the daily lives of millions of you; in the deaf woman who woke up post operatively from a radical mastectomy, devastated because she did not know she was going to have her breast removed because no-one took the time to arrange for an interpreter – she was too embarrassed to say she did not read that language, she spoke a different language, and she signed the consent form. The lessons are in the shop owner who was driven out of business, indeed driven out of town because his community believed he had AIDS – he didn't have AIDS; in the young man who was denied his heart's calling to become a priest because the church said, 'sorry, people with epilepsy can't be priests in the Catholic Church'. Parenthetically, that is the story of our member of Congress who introduced the bill – Tony Coelho. The lesson is in the young man in Chicago, a film-maker, a cameraman, 20 years Hollywood film experience, wounded on the job in an electrical accident, facially disfigured from burns, shows up on a job one day, as he had for 20 years and told, 'sorry, we no longer need a cameraman for this shoot', only to get home and the same day find out that his best friend, another cameraman, had been called back to the site because they did not want a person with facial disfigurement shooting in the movie because it might disrupt the actors' ability to act. The lessons are in your unemployment rate; the lessons are in your stairs and in your stares.

Discrimination does not know any boundaries, any country of origin. If you are a person with a disability, it feels the same. It fosters the same self-fulfilling prophecy on us, it makes us believe that we cannot do things, that we do not deserve things, that we cannot have families. We accept the stereotypes of the museum director who believed I should not have kids. That is when it is at its worst – when we turn the discrimination inward towards ourselves. Susan Faluti is a feminist author who recently wrote a book called *Backlash*. She states that the backlash is worst when it goes inward, when we become our own enemy and we believe the myths. And do not for a minute think that a backlash has to follow a law. I think you all live in a backlash before you have your law. You have to fight those myths, rip away the mask, the disguises, that hide this, and change the terms of the argument.

Last week I had an interesting visit from a member of Parliament here. I was fascinated to hear how the excuses varied but the tone of voice and, fundamentally, the deeply rooted prejudice was still in there. I do not mean to single out this individual, not at all. But I do mean to say that you can feel it in the room when what you are hearing is rhetoric and excuses and the excuse that occurred to me to be the most challenging for you all was the one that said: the reason why a civil rights bill would not be 'in your best interest' – which I love – is because it would be difficult to pass in this country because you do not have a rights-based society. Well, tell me if you do not have a rights-based society. You can tell who has rights and who has not – that is an excuse, you flip it around on their head. I do not think that African descent people who live in this country would tell you you do not have a rights-based society. The man who was set on fire last night in the park probably would say there was a rights-based society. Indeed I understand that you have rights on the books for people of colour and women. Ironic that, even in this day and age, they are still using that argument that this is not a rights-based society when you have two other minority groups who have rights on the books and you still do not. Is that not the sort of epitome of the status that you are all in.

It was in our country, a country which prided itself on its rights history, that our fundamental civil rights law, the Civil Rights Act of 1964 and the subsequent laws throughout our history had not yet included us. Turn to African-American disabled people in America and ask them if they feel prejudice; they feel double prejudice, among the ranks of their own people they are not embraced. So do not accept it.

I think you have to get to the root of why people continue to tell you, you do not need it, you do not deserve it. Fundamentally I think it is because we struggle against two warring notions of people with disabilities and one we do not even talk about. First is the charity model and I shall say no more about that. Second is what we call the brave and courageous model, where we get honours and awards and medals simply for getting up in the morning.

But, fundamentally, it is the third one that gets me, and that is where we are not even on the map of humanity – the sub-human model. The one that allows injustices to go on unnoticed, undetected, unreported, uncounted and unspoken about, even in human rights violations discussions. We are not even on the map of humanity and fundamentally that is what the Americans with Disabilities Act was about. It is so much more than a law. In fact the legal tool aspect of the ADA is 'somewhat irrelevant'. I shall come back later to explain why I say that.

I do not want to be misunderstood. The legal tool is important. But, much more important than the legal tool in my mind has been the moral mandate, the ethical demand for change. I understand that your efforts up to this point have not started out with a strong statement of principle. I urge you to reconsider that, because if we do not start getting at this level of discussion – the fact that we are not even considered part of the whole – how can we get people to start to unlearn that, to give it up, to go on to embrace us as part of the whole. The fundamental goal of a civil rights bill is not to get the bill and is not to give individual people the right to fight the discrimination, it is to create a real sense of community where we are part of that community, where we enter humankind.

As long as we allow the debate to stay on the level where it is right now – and I see you experiencing this, the same way we did – the level of cost, the level of economics, the level of architectural detail, the level of technology needed – we lose. It is a lose-lose scenario. Now, I will give it to you that you have to have those debates. You have to come in armed with your numbers that refute their numbers and be solid with that. I urge you to turn to our country for some of those numbers; the mythology is enough to boggle your mind. So you need to fight on an economics basis. But, if that is where your discussion stays you will lose, and the reasons you will lose are as follows.

Number one, they have more money to crank out more numbers than you do. Look at what the health insurance industry has just done in America – billions of dollars pumped into a mass media campaign to throw out their facts. So, they will come up with better numbers and more numbers. Number two, when you really take a numbers view of this and look at it long-term, the numbers are on your side. Take your unemployment rate, take your social security dollars. In our country when we worked on the ADA we were comfortable in asserting, and knowing we could support, that we spend $200 billion a year keeping disabled people dependent. When disabled people themselves, through polls we did, said that is not the kind of lifestyle we want, we do not want to be on social security, we want to be working, so you are spending already $200 billion of taxpayers' money on programmes we do not want, we want you to take some of that money and put it into changing the way we do business. That argument, whereas it was helpful, did not win the minds and souls of the corporate America. Why? Because they do not think of things in terms of 10 and 20 and 30 and 50 years; they think in terms of next year's profit, this year's bottom line, and this year and next year there is a cost associated with letting us in, and you cannot escape that – even though the data that we have will argue even that point into the ground.

Take the real cost for accommodations in the workplace, for example. Employers who have been putting accommodations into the workplace in our country find that 69 per cent cost nothing at all.[1] When asked have there been benefits accrued to you for making these accommodations, there is a resounding 'yes'. The resounding yes is in the form of reducing retraining costs or if you are getting rid of one worker and then you have to hire a new worker and develop that person, the benefits are in the cost of workers compensation claims not paid because they are keeping people on the job rather than moving them out. In fact for every dollar spent on an accommodation, there is roughly $15 in returns reported by employers.[2]

So you could win on those arguments but if you stop your game there you will lose. You have to circle back up to the broader principle – it is at that level that politicians and do-gooders have a hard time winning. Believe me, when we start saying the truth about what it is like, they do not want to sit and look you in the face and say, 'you're right, I think you're sub-human'. They do not want to do that.

Every country will find its own way of doing this, so when I was asked to suggest our lessons the first thing I want to say is embrace your own difference from us; do not try to follow our pattern. You need to sum up what you can from our experience. But if we were to pass the ADA in 1994 we would have needed to use a whole different series of tactics. The players have changed, the politics have changed, the economic climate has changed, the administration has changed, a lot has changed, we have grown and matured. So, you cannot use a cook book. Whatever you are doing, as long as you are doing it, you are doing it right because you are in there fighting. If it is not working, try something else. This is one where I think disabled people are masters because we have learned in our own individual lives, what I try to teach my kids – I call it 'try, try, again'. If you cannot figure out how to do something this way, well then you try a different technique. I urge you to just keep reaching into those bags of tricks.

As you do so you need to remember that the problem is a problem of discrimination, and the solution must be a rights-based solution. Why? Because first and foremost the solution comes in building our sense of collective self esteem, building a sense of disability pride. Re-defining ourselves is the first step to real empowerment. The law does not empower us, we empower ourselves. The very struggle that you are going through builds your strength because power is what this is really all about and power is fundamental to real change. Here is a quote from a very early civil rights leader in our American history, Frederick Douglas:

> The whole history of the progress of human liberty shows that all concessions yet made to her august claims have been born of earnest struggle. If there is no struggle there is no progress. The struggle may be a moral one or it may be a physical one or it may be both a moral and physical one but it must be a struggle. Power concedes nothing without demand, it never did and it never will.

So, the most important lesson that we have taken out of our experience is what the struggle for the ADA did for us as a community. It built that sense of community, it taught us that when we unite, and set aside our many differences between blind and deaf and cognitive impairments and wheelchair users, when we could work through that diversity and get to our commonness, we were strong. And it was not without many challenges and bumps along the way; that sense of passionate community carried us through those bumps. There were many little issues that cropped up. For example, what should be the definition of disability. Early on there was the thought that it should be sort of narrow, then we broadened it, then the resistance, the conservative resistance came up to try and trim out the less popular disability types – people who have a history of alcoholism, people with AIDS – and we as a community were tempted many times in the interests of the law to cut out some of the players, and fundamentally we did not, in the very end. There was a player who worked with us throughout most of the debate, a person with AIDS and, midway through this he died, and I think in some regards it was his passing that caused the rest of us to realise that we could not let him down. His rights were every bit as important as the rest of us, and that unity carried us.

The second ingredient that was important was some work done by the National Council on Disability, previously called the National Council on the Handicapped. We had a report that was done by this entity which I now chair, that talked about the problems people with disabilities had in housing, transportation, education and so on. The common theme that walked through each of those areas was the experience of discrimination and the missing solution in most of those areas was a comprehensive civil rights approach. That document bound us together, gave us something to point to and legitimised our struggle. Another ingredient were the allies that we built. We drew out from our core to pull in others; we pulled in professionals, we pulled in families, some of whom had disability members in them, some of whom who did not, the religious organisations, unions. We created a sense of understanding and empathy and attempted to rip apart this wall between 'we' and 'they'. We are they – that is the whole point – this happens to everybody. When you can get people to understand that – that we are not that group, we really are part of this whole – they then start to think in different terms.

Another ingredient were the many prominent members in Congress with disabilities. We did the research to find out who was disabled – many of them were not public – and then we went to them face to face and said, 'God, are we glad to hear you're here', and many of them came out of the closet for the first time and once they did, they understood their power with their peers and used it. They told their stories in hearings to their peers in Congress and their peers said to them, 'God, I never knew. I never knew you went through this.' That made a big difference. We had a bi-partisan coalition of those members, Republicans and Democrats, who in our country came out of the closet and joined our ranks and helped us. We had a campaign of truth to fight the lies, and the truth came not from studies, but from people. People – the power is really in your hands, not in their studies. We initiated a discrimination diary campaign. We asked every disabled person we could possibly reach in America to keep a diary for a day, a week, a month or a year, whatever they felt like, and send that diary to Congress. We collected thousands of discrimination diaries and delivered them to the key members. That was a very empowering move. That brought the common everyday person into the struggle and without the common everyday person in the struggle the brilliant strategists in Washington who were working on the details would not have been able to do this.

We intentionally did a low profile media campaign, meaning we summed up early on that the media was not our friend. In fact they were the perpetrators of the greatest degree of the mythology about disability. We realised that we had a choice of going through them and either trying to change the way they portrayed us – and not many of us had hope we were going to accomplish the change with the critical mass of the media – to get the right message out, or we had the option of putting the same energy in different tactics. So our work with the media was more of a reactionary approach; if there was negative stuff coming out we showed up to fight it, but we did not go out and try to get the media to tell our story because we did not believe that they would do it properly. A lot of people do not know that; they think you have got to use the media. There was an orchestrated decision to not do that, at least at the central level in Washington. At the grass roots level people used slightly different campaigns but in reality our grass roots movement did not have either the money or enough expertise in the media to have it really greatly work to our advantage. So if you are finding that to be a problem, I would worry about it to the extent that the media is causing you problems, but I would not think that you need them on your side necessarily. You might want to try to bypass them and go straight to your members of Parliament.

We had a civil rights history, we had others whose images we could lean on and pull from; you have that here too. I am reminded that one of the first human rights documents, the Magna Carta, came here. We had Section 504 of the 1973 Rehabilitation Act. However, from anybody who has lived in America, Section 504 was not really all that well implemented. So while we had it on the books and could use some of the concepts of reasonable accommodation, undue burden to say that this was not an onerous law, it also did not really fuel us at all.

We had struggles around other civil rights bills that went before us. We had well placed people with disabilities in key positions which was very important. We had political appointees by the Bush administration in high level government positions. We had Justin Dart running around the country, meeting with real disabled people, giving a symbolic focal point to the struggle. And those people got into their roles through political participation, they did not just happen there. They had worked for campaigns and as a return they got high level appointments, and that is the truth. Right now, under the Clinton administration, we have an unprecedented number of bona fide grass roots activists running government – 63 to be exact. We had a president who was willing to sign the bill. But you also need to understand that the climate in which all this occurred defied conventional wisdom. The National Council on Disability which proposed this was a Reagan council of conservative Republicans who proposed the first ADA. And the first ADA – a lot of people do not know this – was much more radical than the one that was ultimately passed by the Democratic Congress. We had a shift in parties and you would have expected a more liberal bill to come out. The original bill which came up during a Republican conservative administration from the National Council on Disability was much more radical but the people, the activists on Capitol Hill, felt we needed a more realistic bill in order to try to get it through – they turned out to be right.

The final thing we had was the moral credibility and I have stressed that already. Now where are we? Where we are now is the implementation phase and, as others have said, it is much more difficult to get the law working for you than it is to get the law passed. The most important thing that it has created for us is an opportunity for dialogue. Probably you will feel this to be true; how many of you can get people to talk with you seriously about stuff? Well now they are talking seriously, they have to, they do not have a choice. And it has opened up the first opportunity for what our real goal is – community – because you are sitting in rooms, big corporate rooms, doing disability awareness training sessions, they are paying us to do these things. Now I should also say there was just a crop of consultants who came out of the woodwork who did not know diddly squat about disability and who made a lot of money out of it and, if we had to do it over again, we would have beefed up on our consulting skills earlier to have been in that position.

The business community did not go bankrupt – I have already mentioned that. In fact many of them have turned out to be some of our most outspoken advocates and they have started to see the value of diversifying their workforce. Our courts have not been tied up in litigation. In fact, although there have been 35,000 complaints filed with the Equal Employment Opportunity Commission, only 25 of them have the EEOC initiated into actual law suits. Now, you know, that is good news and bad news. It tells you something about the need to have more people within those government entities able to handle all the complaints; there has been a staffing shortage, not just for our civil rights but civil rights in general, throughout all the agencies, there are not enough people to handle the complaints. There were 5,000 complaints filed under the Department of Justice which has jurisdiction over two areas; roughly 50 per cent of those have gone the legal course and 50 per cent have been settled. What we are finding is that even before you get to the complaints stage in writing, problems are solved, because they are forced to have the discussion; so ramps are built, their doors are widened or Telecommunication Devices for the Deaf (TDDs) are put in before a complaint is ever filed. Those that do go to the complaints phase are largely filed before they go into court, through negotiation, and those that go into court are mostly being won in our favour. We have an Attorney General who is very committed to enforcement and that has helped a great deal.

The problems we have had with implementation include, first and foremost, getting the word out to disabled people. Last year only 40 per cent of disabled people even knew the ADA existed. It is up to roughly 60 per cent this year, but that means 40 per cent of 49 million people still do not know that they are covered. Getting the word out to others, fighting the mythology; most people think they have to do stuff that the law does not require them to do, so a lot of the tension is eliminated the minute they sit down with folks who have been trained in the law. We had a lot of technical assistance money go out to train disabled people, to help them be implementers, but more was needed. We lacked a major PR campaign and if you get your law passed, I think that is something we would do differently if we could afterwards. We are now initiating one, our Attorney General is doing a whole series of Public Service Announcements right now. They are wonderful, they are short, they say something like, 'putting in ramps is not just a nice thing to do, now it is the law', and then she goes on to say it does not need to be difficult, but it is very impressive.

There is some tension between overlapping laws, laws that relate to workers' compensation or environmental hazards. Sometimes the ADA conflicts with that and it has been a challenge for the courts to decide which one supersedes which. We have heard that some people with disabilities rights are better covered than others, certain emerging disabilities such as environmental illness do not feel as well-protected. There has not been enough money to support litigation for disabled people. The traditional legal resource agencies are not good at disability civil rights, it is new, they have not committed themselves to it, many times they are inaccessible, so that has been a problem. Getting the word to minorities, to people of colour, we have only just started to really initiate that, a lot of our materials are finally getting made into Spanish, for example, and, of course, the backlash climate that I mentioned earlier.

Our real job is still ahead of us. We have to realise that we cannot rest on our laurels. The task of continually fighting the backlash is always with us. It is hard work. We need more and more disabled people involved in this and we have to have a continued real deep, gut-level understanding that this is truly a moral issue. Martin Luther

King wrote an article called the 'Ethical Demands of Integration' where he concludes that you have to reach beyond the letter of the law to the spirit of the law; the letter of the law might cause desegregation but real integration, community, happens in a whole – it does not happen in the court room, it happens in people's hearts and minds, and I think that therein lies our real freedom. When we can start having people's hearts embrace us, understand us, care about us, we make change and I would like to close by sharing with you a remark by our new Assistant Attorney General, an African-American man, during his swearing in. His name is Deval Patrick and he says:

> ... but the unifying theme of our work is quite a bit broader than that, the real and ultimate agenda is to reclaim the American conscience, our true mission is to restore the great moral imperative that civil rights is finally all about. This nation as I see it has a creed. That creed is deeply rooted in the concepts of equality, opportunity and fair play. Our faith in that creed has made us a prideful nation, and enabled us to accomplish feats of extraordinary accomplishment and uplift, and yet in the same instant we see racism and unfairness all around us, in the same instant we see acts of unspeakable cruelty and even violence because of race or ethnicity or gender or disability or sexual orientation. They present a legal problem to be sure, but they also pose a moral dilemma; how can a nation founded on such principles dedicated to such a creed sometimes fall so short? To be a civil rights lawyer you must understand what the law means. But to understand civil rights you must understand how it feels. How it feels to be hounded by the uncertainty and fear, about whether you will be fairly treated. How it feels to be trapped in someone else's stereotype, to have people look right through you. To understand civil rights you must understand that the victims of discrimination feel a deep and helpless pain and ask themselves bitterly the very question of morality I just posed. And what will be our answer? Will we sit back and claim that we have no answer or that it is not our business to devise one? Will we shrink from the moral dimension of our work?'

We will not shrink, and neither will you.

References

1 P Blanck, *Communicating the Americans with Disabilities Act: A Case Report on Sears, Roebuck and Co.*, Northwestern University, 1994

2 President's Committee on Employment of People with Disabilities, *Job Accommodation Network: Accommodation Benefit/Cost Data*, Morgantown, 1993

10 Disability, discrimination and local authority social services 1: the social services context

Ray Jones

Clare Evans (the author of Chapter 11) and I are here independently, although we are both working in Wiltshire. One point I want to make by way of introduction is that our two chapters have something of a different feel from the others. They are quite specific, being about social services and about only one area of the country, Wiltshire. What is more, I am the only contributor who has managerial responsibility for the delivery of services, and that determines some of the perspectives I bring and some of the comments I make.

The legislative background
First, I want to set the background framework for the issues I want to explore. The framework in which we are all having to operate is the framework of trying to work together around the theme of 'rights', but also within the reality of rationing. The legal context goes back to 1970 and the Chronically Sick and Disabled Person's Act and, in particular, Sections 1 and 2 of that Act; Section 1 giving a requirement to local authorities to identify disabled people within their area, and requiring that information is provided to disabled people about the services which are available. Section 2 of the 1970 Act is about providing services as of 'right' and based on a duty of the local authority to people who are disabled who need those services.

The judgements which have come out around Section 2 have made it quite clear that decisions taken should take no account of the availability of resources. The requirement, the duty, is that local authorities provide the service regardless of whatever budget, whatever funding, is available.

The second major item of legislation that is part of the background, the framework in which we are operating, is the 1986 Disabled

Person's Act. Several of the aspirations of the Act have not been fulfilled in the sense that they have not been enacted by central government. These sections are very much about representation for people with disability, to allow them themselves, or through advocates, to make their wishes and their needs known, and to be able to canvass to have those needs met.

Secondly, with regard to the 1986 Act, there is the outstanding requirement – outstanding in the sense that central government has again not enacted this section – that the local authority provide written statements to disabled people and their representatives about their needs as they were assessed by the local authority. As we all know, central government has not as yet enacted Sections 1, 2 and 3 of the Disabled Person's Act.

To some extent we might see this as having been overtaken by the 1990 National Health Service and Community Care Act. First, I would particularly note the requirements within the 1990 legislation that the local authority has a duty to assess needs. Second, the local authority has a duty to decide on what services should then be provided to meet those needs and, third, there is then the requirement that the local authority provides information to the disabled person about the services to be provided.

This does leave, however, the contentious issue of unmet need. This relates to the difference between needs being assessed, as required by the 1990 Act, and the 1970 Act requirement that local authorities have a duty to provide a range of services as required by individuals. The 1990 Act, and the government guidance which supports the Act, emphasise 'needs-led assessments', and the 1970 Act emphasises a wide range of services which must be available if required to meet someone's needs. The government has fudged the issue about resources not being available to meet all the needs identified, and we are still expecting that at some stage clarification is likely to have to be sought through the development of case law and through the process of judicial reviews.

But the good news is the response that local authorities are looking to give within the context of this uncertain situation: 86 per cent of social services departments are intending to record, and to report back publicly, the extent of unmet assessed need. Secondly, 59 per cent of local authorities are adopting a policy of giving written assessments back to individual disabled people, and based on the individual assessments there will be a statement of services which can be provided and also a recording of where services are unable to be provided.

That opens the way for legal challenge, but it also reflects a commitment to openness and honesty.

Within the legal framework there are, therefore, a number of issues arising. One of the key issues is around rationing and within the jargon which is developing around rationing – the jargon of eligibility criteria and of priorities for service. One of the positive aspects as to how local authorities are addressing the dilemma of rights and rationing is the explicitness of making available public information about what services a local authority is able to provide within the funding that is available.

This relates to the recording and reporting of unmet need, and it also relates to making explicit decisions around 'gate keeping' access to resources. The reason that I think it is important that local authorities move in this direction is that this is not only about personal issues, and nor is it just about professional issues. In essence we are talking about political issues, and those need to be put in the political arena. One way of making these political issues explicit, for example about the extent of resources available, is to make sure that information is out in the public arena.

However, we should not be totally blinkered by focusing on only the issue of rationing of services and the extent of the resources available. Clearly, there are not adequate resources available to meet all the needs being identified. However, within Wiltshire for example, this financial year the social services department will have a financial turnover of £75m. This does raise the issue of how we are using resources that are available within Wiltshire – the 3,500 staff, the £75m, and the 110 locations for social services within the county.

Recasting the framework
This moves on to the second major theme I want to consider. Without wanting in any way to minimise the issue about the extent of resources available, there is also the issue of how the available resources are being used.

Managerially, there is a danger of seeing the resources as being those of the social services department or those of the county council. But to recast the framework, to change our framework of understanding, we ought to be moving from thinking about resources being in the ownership of the county council or in the ownership of professional workers to thinking about the resources available as increasingly being in the control and ownership of disabled people.

This would include asking the questions: who sets the policy and service agenda, who determines the pattern of services which should be available, and who determines what issues should be given greatest attention?

Again, traditionally, the approach would have been that it is social services managers and politicians who set the framework, who decide on priorities, and who control the shape and distribution of resources. Increasingly we are looking, within Wiltshire, to seeing the use and shape of resources being determined by people who need to use the services.

This raises the issue of how flexible, sensitive and responsive are the services which are available. A number of organisations are going through major structural change, with the introduction of a separation of service purchasing and service provision. Again, new jargon is being invented as we talk about the separation of service commissioning and care management from service provision.

I do not see this just as managerial games-playing and playing around with organisational structures. I do see this as an opportunity to try to free up money within social services, and maybe within other agencies as well, which can be available for discussion with service users about how they want their needs to be met and the pattern of services they personally want to have available.

But there is a further stage to which we should be moving, from people having a choice as to how they have their needs met to a recognition that many people also want to have control over the services and the assistance that they require. This challenges social services departments and paid professional employees to redefine their role. While social services do have a responsibility for rationing, and for assessment and service management, there is another role which begins to loom large. This requires the development of an expertise in enabling.

There are traditions within social work, and within the other professions within social services departments, which would suggest that we already ought to have an expertise in enabling. However, the reality is that the experience, as I understand it, of many disabled people is that they find social services are sometimes far from enabling.

And that moves me on to think about what is happening within Wiltshire. Figure 1 shows how we are increasingly seeking to understand our responsibilities. This is a diagram which is in regular use in the Wiltshire social services department. It has been used in trying to recast the framework in Wiltshire and it has been used in staff training,

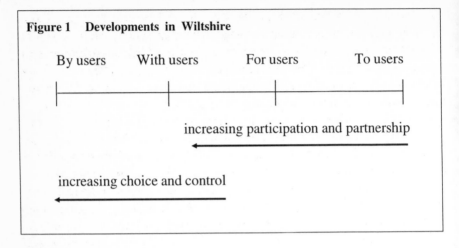

Figure 1   Developments in Wiltshire

By users   With users   For users   To users

increasing participation and partnership

increasing choice and control

and at conferences and workshops involving social services, service users and other agencies.

What Figure 1 shows is a continuum where at one end service users have very little control or say over the services that they receive through to, at the other end of the continuum, services which are directly controlled and determined by service users.

The contemporary discussion around this continuum tends to centre around the theme of participation and partnership. However, there is a further step to be made and that is from participation and partnership through to choice and control by users. I do not declare that we are anywhere near achieving the aspiration of those service users who want control of the services to meet their needs, but we have an increasing understanding that this is the direction in which we should be moving.

The ADSS agenda

As well as decribing what is happening in Wiltshire, I want to reflect briefly on some of the issues identified, and action being taken, by the national Association of Directors of Social Services, and particularly by its Disabilities Committee.

These include, for example, supporting the Bill of Civil Rights; campaigning for cash payments; encouraging across all authorities in the United Kingdom the recording and publication of information about unmet need; and the publication of information about explicit rationing criteria. It is not surprising that the Association of Directors of Social Services also sees as one of its responsibilities, with others, to campaign for adequate funding, both in relation to the community care transfer from social security, but also with regard to long stay hospital closure programmes to make sure that money does not drift away from services. There is also the issue of how criticisms and complaints are responded to within social services, with an increasing thrust to see criticisms and complaints as constructive and positive and requiring an open response.

Lastly it is recognised by the Association of Directors of Social Services that there is a responsibility not just to keep a focus on what is happening within the social services but also what is happening elsewhere within the context of social policy. This includes commenting on, and challenging, changes with regard to Disabled Facilities Grant; changes in social security entitlement; and changing policies with regard to entitlement for health services. One particular issue on which I am sure we are all trying to keep a close eye on is a recent statement in the draft guidance about continuing care where it is suggested that health services should, *within available resources,* have responsibilities with regard to continuing care.

Developments in Wiltshire

But I would like to reflect a little further on what is happening within Wiltshire. Figure 2 shows some of the particular issues to which we are giving attention in Wiltshire.

These include, for example, giving attention to employment in social services. In Wiltshire we are no better, or possibly even worse, than some other employers in terms of employing disabled people. In Wiltshire social services disabled people are known to make up 3.3 per cent of the workforce. I am not sure whether that sounds good or whether it sounds bad, but the reality is that it is quite awful, because within that 3.3 per cent there are 110 workers who are working in two sheltered workshops. We have looked towards trying to re-pattern the resources away from a heavy dependence on sheltered workshops to supported placement provision and integrated employment provision in the community more generally. However, quite strong recent campaigns led to the two workshops remaining open.

If the workers in the sheltered workshops are not included in the overall figures the position for Wiltshire social services is that disabled people make up 1.7 per cent of the workforce. We are monitoring this very strongly, and are taking a number of initiatives around recruitment and retention which are not different from what a number of other organisations will already be taking forward. These include, for example, checking that person specifications are not unfairly

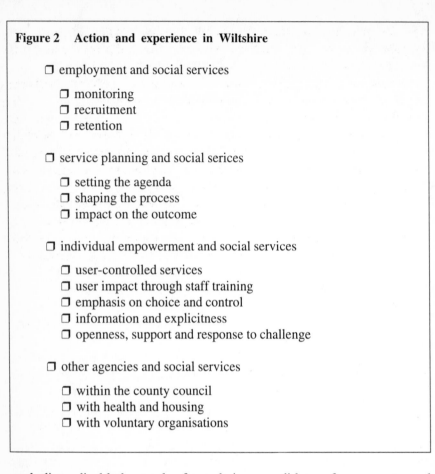

Figure 2   Action and experience in Wiltshire

❏ employment and social services

    ❏ monitoring
    ❏ recruitment
    ❏ retention

❏ service planning and social serices

    ❏ setting the agenda
    ❏ shaping the process
    ❏ impact on the outcome

❏ individual empowerment and social services

    ❏ user-controlled services
    ❏ user impact through staff training
    ❏ emphasis on choice and control
    ❏ information and explicitness
    ❏ openness, support and response to challenge

❏ other agencies and social services

    ❏ within the county council
    ❏ with health and housing
    ❏ with voluntary organisations

excluding disabled people from being candidates for a post, and ensuring that people with a disability, if they choose to declare the disability to us, are guaranteed an interview if they meet the requirements within a person specification. We have also recently focused on equal opportunities training, and positive access and action, throughout the social services department.

The next theme on which I would want to focus is service planning and social services. This does raise the issue of who sets the agenda, who shapes the process by which we consult and who actually leads the consultation about services and policy. Is it social services undertaking consultation, or is the consultation user-led? Increasingly we are delivering on our commitment to open consultation, with the shape and process of consultation being determined more and more by service users. We are also trying to influence our colleagues in other agencies and settings to engage more fully and openly with service users, and not to assume that, for example, voluntary organisations necessarily reflect the view of service users unless they are user controlled.

Finally, by way of summary, if I was asked to very briefly say what we are looking towards in Wiltshire it is acknowledging – within the new management speak – who is the major stakeholder, and who has got the biggest interest in the issues we are addressing. Essentially it is recognising that it is service users who are the major stakeholder. Secondly, it is acknowledging the expertise held by service users. This requires, thirdly, that within social services we need to redefine our role, and to develop expertise, so that we focus on our role as enablers. And finally, all of this recognises that it requires a major culture change for many social services organisations. This is the road that we are beginning to move along in Wiltshire and elsewhere.

11 Disability, discrimination and local authority social services 2: the users' perspective

Clare Evans

In discussing developments in Wiltshire social services, the particular focus that I can bring from Wiltshire Users Network is the opportunities that the community care legislation has given us as service users to influence services for change and remove some of the barriers to participation. I think there is also a perspective from disabled people and from our role and our experience in the Users' Network about the role that social services departments can play in enabling that to happen.

Our organisation is a totally independent user-controlled organisation; 75 per cent of our management committee are service users, and we are resourced by our service agreement – a legally binding service agreement – with social services for the sum of £58,000 with the two aims of facilitating direct links between service users and the social services department providing a network of support for service users countywide. Membership is free to all service users in Wiltshire, including potential users and ex-users. But the particular perspectives which prevail – and from where we get our energy – are the disability movement and the psychiatric survivor movement. We have 350 contacts on our mailing list. Some of these are individual users and others are contacts in user groups of all kinds. We have also just received funding of £25,000 on our annual grant from the Wiltshire and Bath Health Commission.

It is important to us that our involvement is based on our terms and within a background of rights: the rights that we have as citizens like any others – the democratic right to participate in society and the right to have choice and control over our lives – which must mean that we have as much choice and control as we can over the services we receive. And certainly the one informs the other in the sense that that is what we are aiming at in all the user involvement. It is not to save social services money or make the services more efficient or anything like that (although that will be a spin-off for them). It is to make them more appropriate for all service users' needs. Obviously not everyone wants to join in collective user involvement. But, by hopefully enabling local authorities to learn from users' expertise directly, there is the opportunity for those who do chose to participate to change services for all service users. So user involvement has its place within the wider context of removing barriers to disabled people's participation.

We are very proactive in seeking opportunities for user involvement. We work on the principle that it is a matter of riddling the system with as many user perspectives as possible and you win some and you lose some, but on the whole the more opportunities you develop for user involvement the more impact you can make. The aim is not participation for the sake of it and it is not to save ourselves having to sit at home watching television – which is what sometimes people think you would be doing otherwise. It is actually to bring about change. Users in the Network say, 'what's the point of me going and being involved with that, what effect will it have?' – and they will not go and participate unless they know that they are going to be able to have an effect by giving their perspectives as service users. So it is very much the emphasis of wanting to change the culture, from the dependency that we as people who use social services and health services and other agencies to meet our care needs; from the concept of us being dependent on them to the concept of having our right to independent living in the community and our right to help to achieve that. And it is partly just by participating; we have found that if you bring people who usually work with disabled people together with disabled people themselves, then the stereotypes begin to disappear and users' expertise is recognised. It is also partly that user expertise is being brought directly to bear on services, making it possible for professionals to learn how to change them, to be more empowering.

First, our involvement in purchasing. We have carried out research into need and developed a different model of research by groups of service users meeting together to identify gaps in information provision, for example, and then drawing on the research they did with other service users to make policy recommendations. We are also involved in designing service specifications. We have been involved, for example, in the specifications for domiciliary home care – and one wonders how people, professionals, can write service specifications like that without first learning from disabled people what the issues are; being able to tell people, for example, what tasks you want done and not having the tasks listed for you.

Second, we also get involved with developing policy proposals, being involved right from the start. We do not put much store on consultation, because you cannot affect things when people have already half way decided what is happening. But if you are involved right at the start then there is that opportunity.This was particularly the case perhaps with the Wiltshire Independent Living Fund to which I refer again later.

Third, we have been involved in the development of care management and assessment. Care management was designed to be an empowering process, but most people find it is quite difficult to feel that. What is assessment, for example, and how does the process really support the individual? I think the development of care management in Wiltshire, and the way users have been involved with planning and developing it, has changed it from the sort of very structured questions about what you are not able to do, for example, to the assessment form we have designed now which is much more enabling and builds on what help we need to enable us. That has been important and that direct influence has hopefully improved the process for everyone. Training staff in care management has involved service users at all stages. The model in Wiltshire – because we quickly wanted to involve lots of service users – was about users as equal participants with welfare professionals. We have found that has certain spin offs – although it is not the only model to be followed. We are not up there as tutors that everyone can criticise and reject. But as equal participants, being paid to participate, we can share our expertise with other people in group discussions and so on and that has had quite an impression – particularly when a wide range of users' views are heard. Disabled people have found this kind of involvement particularly empowering because the effect of our involvement in changing professional attitudes is very noticeable.

Fourth, another area of activity has been the development of accessible information. User involvement in information provision is about enabling and working with local authorities to enable them to get the information they provide to service users accessible. If you are the officer in charge of information, the last thing you can do is know what a service user needs to know about assessment; you are inevitably caught up in the system of jargon. So, to have a workshop which brings service users together to write that sort of information is hopefully an improvement on the system. For example, being involved in the training of staff who deliver services like home care managers and so on. I remember taking part in one session and it took a whole morning before one of the senior home carers said, 'so you mean it's not making assumptions about your need'. You know, I think we continually underestimate how difficult it is for people once they are in the system to start from where we are.

Fifth, we also have an involvement in service evaluation. When there are reviews of services, we expect to have users there as part of those working groups from the start in order to bring a users' perspective to bear. It is important to have service users defining the questions to ask when an evaluation is being carried out. For example, if the Inspection Unit are doing a survey about the home care service, then we have a meeting with them first and say what the key issues are in terms of what questions to ask and hopefully that can inform the whole survey. Advising on appropriate methods of research is another issue. Does it always have to be able-bodied people interviewing disabled people or can disabled people have a role to play perhaps in getting a more realistic view of people's views of services. People feel safer giving their real views to people they know will understand, who are seen as independent of services, and who do not have the power to penalise people for their views by taking services away.

In order to achieve effective user involvement and remove the barriers which prevent our participation, social services departments must recognise, value and resource user controlled organisations. We have found in Wiltshire as disabled people that, through our own organisation, we have empowered each other to participate effectively and we are accountable to other users. I am employed by the Network and I am accountable to the management committee of users – and that for us is the essence of user involvement in Wiltshire. It is absolutely key. We get several enquiries a week about our work and I groan when people phone up and say 'I've been appointed to do user involvement' and you say, 'well are you a service user?' – 'no'; 'do you work for a user led organisation?' – 'no'. And it is very difficult to know how to help such people to change the whole system round, to have the opportunity of building on the energy and the expertise of the disability movement, to inform the way services have developed, as we have been able to do in Wiltshire.

Three things follow from users having their own organisations and the recognition of the need for that by social services departments. One is that the agenda becomes a users' agenda and it is possible to start from identified need. It is not a matter of just fiddling about with the services at the edges; you can start at the point of what people need and repattern services accordingly. Second, we can get the good practice right; it is about paying for interpreters to come to meetings, for people to have their transport costs met and so on, and it enables local authorities to avoid tokenism because we can advise them on that too. We network with all the disability groups and individuals that are in touch with the Network in Wiltshire, so we hopefully get as good a cross-section of users' views as is possible. As a group of disempowered people, we feel a responsibility to reach out to marginalised groups. Older people, for example; it is much more difficult for them to participate for all sorts of reasons. People from ethnic minorities are also often marginalised. Third, progress in user involvement depends on trust being developed between users and allies. It has helped us that some of our allies are more senior members of the social services department, but at the same time it is actually quite important to recognise the ongoing imbalances of power and the ongoing tensions and we make sure things are not too cosy. Sometimes there are arguments and sometimes it is quite painful, but it is a matter of moving on once they have happened, learning as we go.

I want to turn now to the process of establishing the Wiltshire Independent Living Fund (WILF) and the role that users have played in that. In fact there have been five different roles.

First, once the social services committee made the decision to place the cash into the community to set up an independent living fund, it was suggested that the network put the department in touch with service users who could develop the policy proposals and the financial criteria from their own experience of independent living. There were eight disabled people enabled by two staff from social services plus one or two voluntary organisation representatives to develop the policy proposals and criteria for the fund. Second, from this grew a proposal for the support service for applicants to the fund to be provided through our network, making use of the user expertise of people already living independently. The support service assists disabled people with the assessment process and with enabling them to employ their own staff directly and so on. Third, also out of the policy proposals grew the idea of the awards being made by a grants panel of disabled people. It was only last week that they made their first decisions about funding; that was a panel made up of disabled people and I think that, in the next financial year, they will be making decisions about £1m worth of funding. Fourth, another way in which users' expertise will be used in connection with WILF is through monitoring the progress of the scheme. The policy group that set it up will be getting in touch with the users of the scheme to make sure that it is working according to their expectations. Finally, the by-product that I guess none of us imagined at the start was that we actually managed to change social services mainstream charging policy to get it in line with the criteria that users had set up. One of the things we recognised as important was people being assessed independently of their partners and we managed to persuade the social services committee that that was a change for the better in their charging policies – which we felt was quite good.

The other area of work which it seems important for social services to enable us as disabled people to do is to run our own services if we choose. We do have opportunities for the Network to do that in the current year as we have got a budget of £250,000 this year to run our own services. Also, we made all the funding applications through the usual joint finance and departmental processes. I think sometimes people say disabled people's organisations should have a level playing field with other independent organisations in bidding for services. But, I am not sure we should not have it tilted in our favour because there is so much expertise in the disabled community that we know we can provide services very well – particularly if it is making use of things that we have real expertise in, such as provision of information, advocacy, and independent living.

There are five services we are running this year. The Patients' Council Project which is based at a local psychiatric hospital; the Information Federation, which has grown out of the knowledge that we have learned about schemes in other parts of the country; there is an Information Drop-in Centre in Salisbury which will be run by disabled people, employing disabled people and so on; the support service for WILF which I have mentioned; and, because of our concern about the lack of participation by people from ethnic minorities in the Network, and the feeling that we were excluding them as we seemed to gain more power, we developed a proposal with allies – which was accepted – to be a Living Options Partnership site, and this is about reaching disabled people in African-Caribbean and Asian communities in Wiltshire and enabling them to access services.

I hope that this demonstrates something of the opportunities that we have had in Wiltshire and the support we should be able to expect from social services departments to enable us to participate in the services we receive.

12 Discrimination and the law: what can legislation achieve?

Ian Bynoe

The recent and continuing campaign for comprehensive civil rights for disabled people has concentrated on legislative solutions with the short Civil Rights (Disabled Persons) Bill being regarded as of fundamental importance and value in the drive to secure lasting social change. There is a confident belief that the approach adopted in this bill is one which is bound to be effective in removing barriers. This chapter examines the usefulness of laws in prohibiting discrimination and providing effective rights of access to equal opportunity and fair treatment. In essence, we shall be probing the questions:

* What distinctive advantages do legal measures bring which non-legislative policies cannot provide?

* What are the ways in which legislative solutions can be formulated and introduced and what is special about 'civil rights' legislation?

* What relevance do these issues have for today's UK campaign and any prospect of forthcoming legislation?

Laws can provide the means to define civil and political relationships in society, and, where these are unequal or are non-existent, to modify or to create them. Movements for social justice make claims for better or fairer treatment not just for individuals but for groups of people, and the reach of the law means that universal approaches are possible – in effect, a legal status in Cornwall can be the same which applies in Camberwell. The law is well used to defining groups of people and attaching rights to such status descriptions. It does it all the time. If such distinctions are complex and highly varied, then laws which have to formulate these may have to be as complicated. Lawyers are also used to working with definitions of behaviour or conduct and to creating institutions to resolve disputes about such conduct. This is not to say that just because the law is chosen as a means of implementing this social policy, only one approach is available or predetermined. Where legislators have already attempted to draft measures to combat disability discrimination they have employed a variety of different means sometimes combining these in one statute. But before we consider them, what do I mean by discrimination. In answering this question I do so from a lawyer's perspective.

I see four distinct types of discrimination and offer these as a comprehensive description. It is something of an analytical tool. There may be situations where categories merge or are found together but these are not common. I preface three of the four classifications with the word 'unfair'. This is not to say that even the concept of 'fairness' is an absolute rule or concept. It is often relative to the precise policies which underwrite the law. As well, we constantly have to remember that some different and clearly less favourable treatment will amount to discrimination but cannot be condemned. In a campaign for social justice, laws which help to define – and extend where possible – the boundary between fair and unfair discrimination will be essential to the task of winning popular support. The four situations are these:

- Unfair direct discrimination: here a person or organisation treats another person less favourably because of their actual or perceived disability in a way or ways which would not be employed in the case of a person without such a real or perceived disability. The person experiencing this treatment would in all respects be able to participate in the activity or role in question. I could choose many examples of this type of discrimination. Many are listed in the recent Liberty/BCODP report on human rights.[1] A holiday camp which refused a booking from a group of people with cerebral palsy; a landlord who banned a disabled skittles team from a pub because he believed some of its members to be 'mentally handicapped'; an employer who refused to hire a qualified blind telesales person because its office was on the first floor and the employer thought that blind people could not walk up stairs. This concept covers stereotypical behaviour where a person experiences less favourable treatment because of have a reputation or history of being a disabled person.

- Unfair indirect discrimination: this occurs when an apparently neutral entry or qualification condition which is non essential has a disparate impact on disabled people which is unfair. It is not immediately apparent that discrimination is going on since there is an illusion that every person is treated the same. The best example which I came across when I worked at MIND was an employer who obliged all employees to participate in a private health insurance scheme, provided as a fringe benefit with the employment. Clearly, a deal had been struck with the insurers on the basis of only defined risks being covered. In that process, the insurers had excluded cover from those with a recent history of treatment for mental illness, even where full recovery had occurred. This requirement for a 'first class' life was incorporated into the recruitment process used by the employer and, of course, had a vastly disproportionate impact on those applying for jobs unable to qualify for such cover. Another – infamous – example will be 'no dogs' rules in taxis or buildings, such as at investitures at Buckingham Palace; or the requirement that someone must possess a driving licence in order to undertake a job which could be performed by someone using other means of transport.

- A third example of unfair discrimination arises where a person or organisation fails or refuses to remove an artificial barrier (physical, environmental, organisational) which prevents another person's participation to the same extent as someone without a disability. Here the unadapted environment is inaccessible to that person but in all other respects they would be able to qualify for or participate in the activity. Where the provision of an interpreter or assistant, the physical alteration of premises – for example, with the adaptation of the telephone system – or the creation of more flexible working arrangements would enable access then a failure to do these things at once appears discriminatory. It will be unfair if the impact – expense, disruption and changes – are reasonable bearing in mind the size and financial viability of the organisation and its access to public funds to do this.

- The last example of discrimination, much quoted by those sceptical of or hostile to the idea of anti-discrimination legislation, arises where the barrier preventing access is insurmountable, the less favourable treatment reckoned to be fair and just. Those who want to rubbish legislative solutions claim that laws will not include such a category and that they will for example require employers to hire people who cannot perform the tasks needed in the job – blind airline pilots. The argument runs that disabled people will gain an unfair advantage from such legislation. I have never seen contemporary laws which are designed to have this effect though positive discrimination measures are not unknown and have their place. Mainly the legislation is concerned to offer means of arriving at the boundary between fair and unfair discrimination and frequently provides ample justification for the former.

Let us now look briefly at some of the approaches which have been taken in law and the options which are available in a UK context.

Statutory duties
Organisations and individuals can have imposed upon them duties which are defined in law. These can be stated in very general or in highly specific terms. Just because the law has imposed a duty, it does not mean that a corresponding right is acquired by the person who is meant to benefit from compliance. If the law wants that to happen it usually has to say so. This is what marks out the civil rights approach which insists that with duties must go corresponding rights. We must not forget, however, that there will be situations where what may be needed is a combination of clear and specific duties together with individual rights of enforcement – you cannot have the one without the other.

General duties
Anyone familiar with recent lobbying on parliamentary legislation will recognise the 'general duty' approach. Where governments come under pressure to respond they often create vague and unenforceable duties. For example, as Bryan Heiser notes in Chapter 5, London Regional Transport must include the needs of disabled people in their transport planning for London.[2]

Specific duties
Here, the law gets down to the detail of what needs to be done and specifies it explicitly. The regulations on access to public transportation passed under powers given by the Americans with Disabilities Act is a good example of this. Anyone familiar with these will know the detailed requirements which they contain. The UK's building regulations come into this category though I am sure that many would argue they are far from being sufficiently detailed, comprehensive or universally applicable. The Quota Scheme is based on this approach. One can see its weaknesses!

Contracting requirements

Contract compliance can offer a means of redressing discrimination or preventing its reoccurrence, and the law can be used to oblige public or private bodies to insist that their contracts guarantee minimum standards, for example, of access. As more and more public services leave public control for the private or quasi private sector, such regulation as is maintained via the terms of franchise contracts or licences will become evermore important. The law can be drafted so as to impose on the regulator a duty to ensure that services are provided without unfair discrimination and if removable barriers exist to access can establish targets and monitor compliance against these. Oftel, for example, could require companies seeking licences to provide telecommunications services to render their facilities technically accessible to those with speech or hearing difficulties.

Individual rights

An alternative or additional approach goes further than simply describing duties in law. It provides individuals with enforceable rights to complain of discrimination. There appear to be two ways of doing this. One sees the same approaches in relation to discrimination on grounds of sex and race.

The 'Human Rights Charter' approach

In Canada, at a national level and in some individual provinces, broad and general human rights declarations have been passed into law protecting disabled persons from discrimination broadly defined. This is one way of trying to be comprehensive. Mechanisms have been established to receive, investigate and adjudicate on complaints of human rights breaches.

The specific rights approach

In the US and in most parts of Australia and now at a Commonwealth level, the legislators have sought to be more specific in defining situations in which discrimination might be judged unfair and ruled unlawful. The legislation is still about human and civil rights but care has been made to recognise the different situations in which they might have to be enforced and to tailor the laws to these differing contexts. This is another approach to drafting comprehensive legislation, but it leads – particularly in the US setting – to very lengthy and complex statutes which rely on subsidiary regulations for much of their practical implementation.

The difference

What this approach adds is the ability for citizens to seek redress when they feel that they have experienced discrimination.They are able, at least in theory, to seek to assert and have accepted their view of justice and fairness instead of having to rely on some state official to do or not do something. This makes the title 'civil rights' distinctive and accurate.

Criminal sanctions

Sometimes the criminal law is employed to prohibit discriminatory behaviour. Social condemnation of such conduct is regarded as so great as to justify the use of criminal sanctions. In South Australia, the Equal Opportunity Act renders it a criminal offence for a service provider or employer to require a person to be separated from his or her guide dog. Tell that to Buckingham Palace!

Enforcement mechanisms

There are a number of different methods of enforcement to choose from. A combination will probably be needed. What will be required is:

- monitoring the effectiveness of the legislation, reporting on this and suggesting amendments to the law, regulations and any codes of practice;

- investigating individual complaints of discrimination,applying the law to these;

- providing assistance to those wanting advice as to how to comply with the law;

- providing assistance to those seeking to enforce their rights by litigation;

- providing specialised bodies to rule on complaints of discrimination – employment, services, access to facilities and transportation.

None of this is new and I am sure that many of you are familiar with these points. I end with some reference to the present UK situation and the essential issues which need to be resolved by those pressing for legislative solutions. The campaign for comprehensive rights will not succeed simply when Parliament passes a law with 'civil rights' in its title. It will have been effective when legislators are persuaded to meet the scale and challenge of the task and to take the trouble to produce effective and wide-ranging laws, whose scope, imagination and complexity are equal to the task.

What are the key issues we should be considering? I identify three:

Who should have new rights – who is a disabled person?

It is essential that any new law should be fairly clear as to whom it is to apply to. Where its cutting edge is blunt the law can be brought into disrepute and conservative judges operating in a system which relies on literal interpretation can have a field-day restricting its scope. Witness the House of Lords decision to remove anyone unable to assert their rights because of learning disability to apply for accommodation under the Housing Act 1985. The ADA gets over the problems of its progressive definition of disability by listing – non exclusively – in regulations a set of medical diagnoses – impairments – which passport a person into the reckoning. To meet the criticism about vagueness such a step may have to be adopted here. To meet the observations about indirect discrimination and perceived disability we need to have examples to demonstrate the flaws in a bill which excludes such situations from coverage.

How does one balance the need for clarity with the need for flexibility?

A major difficulty with anti-discrimination legislation is that it establishes broad rights and duties which have to be applied in a multitude of differing situations. If the legislation sought to offer cast iron rights in every setting it would be very specific and detailed – and governments would never agree to pass such legislation. Therefore there is reliance on regulations or codes, the former mandatory, the latter often advisory. We should start envisaging what such documents should look like and how prescriptive they should be. These need to spring from the experiences of disabled people. Government is entitled to expect the movement to offer detailed and accurate advice on this.

Should there be new – and unprecedented – enforcement powers?

Enforcement is the key. It distinguishes rights from 'two ticks' schemes. There are worrying flaws in the present systems of enforcement. The industrial tribunal scheme is now highly adversarial – professional representation is essential but no legal aid is available. Unions offer this to their members. I guess that many disabled people would not be active union members. Tribunal powers are limited and efforts to increase them via amendments in the House of Lords were defeated.

The area needs a lot more work; some to be devoted to innovation such as the creation of rights for organisations to bring complaints as class or representative actions which would take the impact of judgements beyond the narrow confines of an individual's complaint.

As the campaign moves on we must be utterly realistic about how our laws are made in the United Kingdom. I shall finish with a sanguine reminder of this and how often the Palace of Westminster misses the target as well as the point. Since 1 November 1993, Section 89 of the Leasehold Reform, Housing and Urban Development Act 1993 has been in force. This makes void any lease or tenancy terms which prohibit or restrict the occupation of a dwelling by someone with mental health problems or a learning disability. All very good. As we know, restrictive covenants can be employed to hinder or prevent community care housing schemes. Read this and you think Parliament has dealt with the problem. Read it again and the problems start to emerge. It does not apply to freehold properties – it would have no application in the infamous Bath case. And, worst of all, it does not render unlawful a refusal to grant a lease on grounds of disability. So a lease cannot restrict occupation on grounds of disability but those who want to discriminate can simply refuse to grant the lease in the first place. We have a long way to go yet!

References

1   BCODP/Liberty, *Access Denied: Human Rights and Disabled People,* National Council for Civil Liberties, 1994
2   London Regional Transport Act 1984

13 From charity to rights: a disabled person's journey

Bob Findlay

Our journey as disabled people has been a long and complicated one with many diversions on the way; yes, many cul-de-sacs too. We know only too well that have not yet reached our destination and the struggle ahead is still going to be an uphill one.

The history of our struggle, like those of many other oppressed groups, has not just been unrecorded; it has been distorted by time and by numerous misrepresentations. A few disabled people have tried to put together the jigsaw pieces which make up our history over the last 130 odd years and, in so doing, have argued that we have come together as a distinct and oppressed social group. A large part of our history relates to the differing roles played out by the state and charities in shaping our lives – they have helped defined who we are, what we are and, from their point of view, what we are considered to be capable of.

I believe it is possible to say that we – both as individuals and as a collective social group – have a dual identity. On the one hand, we have the identity as 'the disabled' (sic) – this poor group of wretched creatures not able to look after themselves; dependent on goodwill, state hand-outs, and, of course, charity! Prior to the nineteenth century we had Lady Bountiful with her handouts and in the 1980s there was Esther Rantzen – can you spot the difference? The social construction of 'the disabled' legitimated the creation of material barriers which have kept us marginalised and excluded; encouraged to be passive, dependent, not knowing really who we were except in the guises that they were happy to hand down to us.

We also see from the nineteenth century onwards how social policies have dealt with us as a social group. I have a problem here because like everyone else I am affected by my own personal politics;

as a socialist, I continue to argue for the defence of the welfare state, but as a disabled person, I am aware that the type of welfarism coming from the state and charities has not always been at the forefront of meeting our true requirements. It could be suggested that, if anything, welfarism has helped to reinforce our experience of dependency.

It is almost paradoxical that we have actually seen the disability movement flower at the moment when the shift in culture is away from calls for universal rights and state interventions towards the type of individualism encouraged by Thatcherism and the creation of social policy which is governed by the dictates of 'market forces'. The politics surrounding community care and the disability movement's demand for independent living will, in my opinion, expose further contradictions within notions of a welfare state whether from a conservative or social democratic perspective, and I think this needs to be examined.

The slogan 'rights not charity' is not just about challenging those good-doers who rattle tins as a means of dealing with us; the challenge goes deeper because it is concerned with the actual culture in which we have had to live. In this sense, 'rights not charity' is not merely a slogan and neither is it just another political demand; it is about creating a framework for understanding ourselves and awakening our awareness of our second identity.

I said we have a dual identity. This second identity is about understanding who we are and what it is that unites us. What unites us is not the particular impairment or condition that we might have, but rather, the implications arising from having impairments in a society that fails to address the needs and interests of people with impairments. It is precisely how society organises that helps to determine the discriminatory barriers we encounter. We need an understanding of what brings us together, creates our unity, and forges our identity as 'disabled people'. Our identity as 'disabled people' has to be articulated through the recognition of the distinctive nature of the oppression we face.

To recognise that we experience a distinct form of oppression is not enough; we have to go beyond this point and learn from other oppressed groups. Our second identity, as an oppressed social group, contains within it fragments from all other oppressed groups; the membership of our social group brings together a myriad of experiences. We must therefore recognise the connections and disconnections that can be made with other oppressed groups. We must examine how these experiences have shaped our awareness, our identities, and the closeness or the distance we have as individuals or as fragments of our social group, with and from, non-disabled people who might be from another oppressed group we identify with.

Although we have seen our history stand a hundred years or so, we still have the political task of reclaiming it. How many of you are aware that in the 1930s the National League of the Blind – a disabled trade union organisation – marched across the country with a big banner which proclaimed 'justice not charity'. Today, of course, we say 'rights not charity' but the message remains the same. We have seen in the last 20 years a reawakening of the issue of justice.

We have seen disabled people question their position in society and recognise that the issue of disability is about denial: a denial about our identities, a denial of our opportunity to participate fully within society. We have seen this recognition articulated through two processes. First of all there has been a radical critique of how society oppresses us – this is what is known as the personal tragedy approach to disability. Through this critique we began to see how we as an oppressed group could reinterpret our position within society and identify the encountered barriers. In other words, we developed the social oppression approach towards disability.

I must confess that sometimes I get frustrated with the language and definitions associated with 'disability'. Disabled people in the movement talk about the 'social model' and it is assumed that we have a common understanding of this approach – but are we being totally honest? Personally, I think the term 'social model' is too vague; we should clearly state that we are talking about a form of social oppression. I think we have got to be careful not to let the concept of oppression slip out of our language and analysis of the barriers we face. To talk about the social model can depoliticise in many ways the issues we should be concerned about. It needs putting back on the agenda and we must say 'damn it' to those who hit us with this nonsense about us wanting to be politically correct etcetera.

I believe that disabled people, through the idea of disability as social oppression, began to re-evaluate who they were, where they were positioned within society and where they wanted to go on their journey. The focus was on what it was that really disabled us and to debate what the 'disabled' identity meant to us. It seems an age ago – it was actually about 23 years – when we were having all these debates with the Disablement Income Group about whether or not we could reduce the issue of disability to the extra cost that we face and whether we needed a national disability income. How far we have come between now and then! During this period we have learnt from the struggles of our American brothers and sisters about their civil rights activities. There was also the wider political agenda: the fight against apartheid in South Africa, the black civil rights movement, the anti-Vietnam war demonstrations, the women and the gay liberation movements all fed into our development of the concept of liberation politics. We began to understand more concretely that we were talking about issues like power and control. Who controls our lives? How do we make decisions about the kind of lifestyles we want to live as disabled people?

In 1981, the International Year of Disabled People, we saw two major events: the formation of the Disabled People's International and of course, in Britain, the British Council of Organisations of Disabled People. BCODP's membership has grown to over 100 and they have been involved in developing a greater understanding of the issues that affect us as disabled people. These issues are not just about legislation and civil rights but include questions around independent living. Perhaps their greatest contribution has been the development of the self-organisation of disabled people – building up our membership, developing the day to day practice of disabled people – because these things have helped to feed into how we have increased the momentum behind the demand for civil rights.

If you look at the early bills our influence on them was limited. Generally speaking, it was the large charities who organised the lobbying and had the ear of the MPs who did the bargaining on our behalf. Disabled people were like the Grand Old Duke of York's army – they wheeled us into the lobby and they wheeled us out again; meanwhile, the MPs' hands went up and out went successive bills – that was the process. Five years ago, through the development of our experience, we began to become more involved in making an intervention in the process. The creation of Voluntary Organisations for Anti-Discrimination Legislation gave disabled people a more central role in campaigning for our own rights. We began to develop our own agenda, our own expertise, on the issues.

We also saw disabled people take more radical steps, thus capturing the feeling of anger that is out there. The march in 1989 on Scott's office at the Elephant and Castle and the sit down protest there introduced to Britain an example of civil disobedience by disabled people. I believe that was a turning point and a watershed for civil rights campaigning. Now we have seen a new development, not just with the support we got for the Civil Rights Bill, but the fact that we launched the Rights Now Campaign. This brought together and caught the imagination of disabled people because if fused together the identity of a struggle around a demand. It was simple; it was straightforward; it hit home at the very heart of what we want, and therefore it gave us a focus that talk of anti-discrimination legislation would never do.

We have come a long way this year but there are danger signs ahead. The government came close to losing the ground to us. We know this and so do they. It is vital for them to recapture some of that ground. The publication of that horrid, toothless consultation document – *Measures to Tackle Discrimination* – is their reluctant acknowledgement that legislation is inevitable. After a hasty retreat, they have launched a counter-offensive and at the earliest opportunity they will introduce some form of piecemeal and ineffective legislation. This will not be what we have asked for, not what we need, and certainly not what we want. But how will we deal with this situation? We have to recognise that we need a strategy. We cannot put all our eggs in one basket. We cannot just say we do not want it, ask for a vote against it, then turn our backs and carry on as if it is business as usual. That is what I would call political posturing of the worse kind. What we have to do is to bring back our own bill, but we have also got to respond to their bill; what is good for goose is good for the gander.

First of all, to take a leaf or two out of their book – if they can say to the IRA and Sinn Fein, there is the Downing Street Declaration but there can be no renegotiation of it, then so can we. We might tinker with our own bill, which advocates comprehensive legislation, but we will do so to improve it; what we will not do is move away from that position. No compromising on principles. Secondly, when they do introduce their bill then again we must amend it. We must make their bill look a mirror image of our own. We have got to gear up the MPs who support us to put new amendments in, to fight the case, to filibuster, and if needs be, talk it out; all the tactics they can use, we should urge our supporters to use. If the government can defend the interests of their 'friends' then we must defend our people with equal vigour.

Lastly if we do not succeed – if it looks as if that bill might go through and if it is still not what we want – then I am afraid we have to take stock of where we are on the road. We have come this far: it is too far to turn back, and too far to get carted off down a cul-de-sac. We might not get everybody on our side. But, at the end of the day, although we do want partnerships and we do want to work with people, in the final analysis we must look after ourselves. We must defend our own interests because I am afraid nobody else will do it for us. We have had a history of people 'doing' for us – and look where that has got us!